A TASTE OF
TRADITION

Dedicated to my mother
Who taught me **"HOW"** _; to_
my father, who taught me **"WHY"** _;_
And to my husband, who held my hand.

Other books by Ruth Sirkis:

Popular Food from Israel, in English, French, Spanish, German, Russian and Japanese
Cooking with Love, in Hebrew, 1975
Children are Cooking, in Hebrew, 1976
Kosher Gourmet Chinese Cooking, in Hebrew, 1979
Cooking with Pleasure, in Hebrew, 1982
Paprika, The Jewish way of Hungarian Cooking, With Joseph Lapid, in Hebrew, 1986
From the Kitchen with Ease, in Hebrew, 2001
International Savoury Pies, in Hebrew, 2002
International Salads, in Hebrew, 2003
Cooking in the Internet, in Hebrew, 2004

A TASTE OF TRADITION

The How and Why
of
Jewish Gourmet
Holiday Cooking

BY RUTH SIRKIS

Color Photographs by RAFAEL SIRKIS

R. SIRKIS PUBLISHERS LTD.,
TEL AVIV, ISRAEL

Cover Photograph: POT OF PLENTY – Pot Roast with Pleny of Vegetables
Recipe on page 12

First Edition: Ward Ritchie Press, Los Angeles, California, 1972
Second Edition, Zmora Bitan Modan, Tel Aviv, Israel, 1978
Third Edition, Bayit VaGan Publishers, Tel Aviv, Israel, 1979
Fourth Edition, R. Sirkis Publishers, Ramat Gan, Israel, 2004

This book is partially based on, and developed from, material originally published
and copyrighted by the Jewish Telegraphic Agency, Inc. of New York, and
syndicated by them to the Anglo-Jewish Press, in the years 1968 to 1972. It also
includes recipes and color photos, originally published in AT Magazine, part of
Maariv Group, Tel Aviv.
The patterns of bunny and chick, on page 53 courtsey of Durkee Company.

Library of Congress Catalog Card Number, of the first edition: 72-173237
ISBN of this Edition: 965-387-069-6
Israeli Catalog Number: 46-1105

Published by R. Sirkis Publishers Ltd., www.sirkis.co.il
131 Bialik Street, P. O. Box 3561, Ramat Gan 52523, ISRAEL
Telephone: +972-3-751-0792, Fax: +972-3-751-3750. E-Mail: info@sirkis.co.il

Cover photograph by Hanan Sadeh, all other photographs by Rafael Sirkis
Book designed by Rafael Sirkis and Joseph Simon
Cover designed by David Tartakover

CONTENTS

INTRODUCTION

The earliest and fondest memories of my childhood in Israel are connected with Holidays and their food. The whole family gathered on Passover at my grandparents' home, and the taste of fresh crisp *matzah;* the glow of *Hanukkah* candles on wintry nights, and hot potato *latkes;* masqueraded children parading Tel-Aviv streets on sunny *Purim* days, and sweet *hamantashen.* Life seemed to revolve around the Jewish Holidays with their beautiful rich tapestry of themes, making the year a continuous melody of festivities. As a child I took them for granted, as I took my mother's cooking. She is a 'natural' and turns out the best *gefilte fish, tcholent* or *lekach* without any cookbook.

As time progressed I realized the importance of tradition. Backed with some knowledge in psychology and sociology, which I gained at the Hebrew University of Jerusalem, I clearly saw how Holidays helped in molding the personality of individuals and a nation. It is those Holiday dinners and gatherings, specialty foods and festive atmosphere that introduce youngsters to the Jewish history and heritage in a tangible way; that strengthen their bonds with their families; and provide a reassured personality and clear sense of identity. Now, being a mother myself, trying to raise three young children in this complicated, confused world of ours, I discovered a new face in tradition. I cannot but be aware of the fun, and togetherness we all share on Holidays and *Shabbat,* when home and family mean so much more.

It is this special quality of Holiday atmosphere that I want to share with you. The book's chapters follow the Jewish Holidays as they follow the rhythm of changing seasons. Each chapter contains stories about the Holiday's meaning, customs and traditions, and complete menus to create a total festive feeling. Some of the dishes on these menus are outstanding and will rank high with the gourmet; and many are colorful with a distinctive 'eye-appeal' to delight the creative cooks.

A TASTE OF TRADITION has been designed with today's life style in mind. Diet awareness and children's participation account for moderate portions, and for meals that are intended to satisfy rather than stuff. The menus and recipes lend themselves easily to modern entertaining. There are tempting appetizers, exciting main dishes, and glorious desserts. You may also mix and match, consulting the Recipe Index, to create your own menus for dinner parties, receptions and casual get-togethers. For children's birthdays make use of the beautifully decorated, unusual cakes. The book observes the Jewish dietary laws. (For more about the laws of *Kashrut* and how to use the book to comply with them, please turn to page 122.)

In choosing recipes to represent the multitude of Jewish delicacies I naturally started with my own favorites. Some, such as *tzimmes* or *kneidlach,* I learned in my mother's kitchen *(Ashkenazi)* and others, spicier, such as fish in tomato sauce or artichokes for Passover, from my mother-in-law *(Sephardic).* My professional interest in food, as writer and food editor in Israel and in the United States, has acquainted me with international cookery. I have included some of these foods *(quiche, mousse,* pizza, etc.) adapted to a kosher kitchen, as well as recipes which were particularly liked by my readers on both sides of the ocean.

Ruth Sirkis
Los Angeles, February 1972.

INTRODUCTION TO THE 21ST CENTURY EDITION

Thirty two years after it was originally published by Ward Ritchie Press in Los Angeles, there is still a lively trading going on, in used copies of A TASTE OF TRADITION, in the pages of the world's largest book selling organization – Amazon. Two additional publishing companies in Israel, which printed the book in the 80's, are also no longer in business. But the book apparently has a life of its own. The edition you are holding in your hands is published by my own publishing company – R. Sirkis Publishers Ltd., simply because there is so much demand for it.

Its brother book, POPULAR FOOD FROM ISRAEL, which was also originally published in 1972 in Los Angeles, by BUN Publishing, had a similar, yet different fate. It became the most popular souvenir Israeli cookbook. I commissioned the translations of the book into French, Spanish, German, Russian, and Japanese. Color pictures of all the dishes and of interesting Israeli sights, both culinary and general, were added. And now all these versions are sold, side by side in tourist souvenir shops, and airports in Israel.

But most of my activities in those years were concentrated in the Hebrew language. I wrote 10 additional major cookbooks, and published about 100 more – my own books and the books of others. Some were original titles, written in Israel, and some were translated from English, French, German and Italian. All of them comply with the Jewish dietary laws. Acting as the chief editor of my publishing company I supervised translations, adaptation to Israel, elaborate food photography, funny sketches and beautiful artworks. These were indeed wonderful years.

My current pet project is the Internet, which opens new vistas. I ventured into food video production; established a weekly Internet newsletter, for subscribers, which includes video, and is highly interactive; and inaugurated my own English-Hebrew web-site: www.sirkis.co.il. Please come and visit!

Communication with my readers also changed over the years, and became much easier. When the book was first published in 1972 the only way was regular mail. In the 80's facsimile became a faster and simpler way of communication. Today I can be reached even better and almost at no cost by e-mail to my box: Ruth@sirkis.co.il

Ruth Sirkis
Ramat Gan, September 2004

APPLE AND HONEY STRUDEL (recipe on page 16), on the
left, and **HONEY CAKE** (recipe on page 13), on the right,
are shown with their traditional ingredients. The legend
on the card reads in Hebrew, Shanah Tovah, which means
Happy New Year.

I

ROSH HASHANAH: DISHES WITH BEST WISHES

THE HEBREW WORD *Rosh* means 'head' or 'beginning'; *Hashanah* means 'the year.' Together they say 'Beginning of the New Year'. Jewish people welcome the new year on an introspective note, evaluating their deeds of the one just ended. They ask God's blessings for the year to come through worship, prayer, charitable donations and by reaching out to their fellow men.

Rosh Hashanah is a two-day holiday during which it is customary to pray frequently, listen to the *Shofar* (ram's horn), and personally wish friends *Shanah Tovah* (have a good year): a year of health, better understanding among people and, above all, peace on earth.

The holiday has deep roots in the Jewish tradition and the foods with which it is associated have special meanings and definite reasons for being served. Their color, shape or type expresses a particular wish for a good year to come. These foods may vary from one Jewish community to another, according to regional tastes or the ingredients available, but they are used to signify the same things: the yearning for a better year.

Foods normally included on *Rosh Hashanah* menus in much of the world are:

Fish—a symbol of fertility; usually served with the head on, indicating the desire to 'get ahead'.

Carrots—always sliced in rounds to resemble gold coins in shape and color.

Challah—slightly sweet, raisin-dotted and baked round to represent the longing for a full and wholesome year.

Fruit and vegetables—served in abundance as omen for a plentiful harvest.

Honey and apples—it is customary to dip apple slices or bits of *challah* in a small dish of honey to signify hopes for a sweet new year.

Rosh Hashanah dinner is not just another meal; it is an integral part of the Jewish New Year observance. With family and friends joined, everyone experiences a particularly strong feeling of brotherhood.

[9]

The occasion is special in every way. The table is set with the family's most beautiful linen, china, silver and crystal and dinner is prepared with particular care to leave no doubt about the importance of this holiday.

The festive atmosphere of *Rosh Hashanah* evening lingers throughout the year, and the memories of the family enjoying the holiday dinner together accompany youngsters throughout their life.

Planning A Successful *Rosh Hashanah* Dinner

Two complete *Rosh Hashanah* menus are offered in this chapter. Although they vary in preparation, flavors, shapes and textures, they are structured as traditional meals. Each is a gourmet feast composed of favorite specialties intended to be relished in a leisurely manner; both include the traditional *Rosh Hashanah* well-wishing foods: fish, carrots, *challah,* apples, honey and vegetables.

We suggest that you decorate the centerpiece with apples and have candles ready to light at sunset. Put wine on the table for *Kiddush,* wine benediction, along with small dishes of honey surrounded by sliced apples and two *challot* covered with a napkin for *Hamotzi,* the bread benediction. Provide a knife for cutting the *challah* after the benediction and encourage everyone to dip bits of the *challah,* as well as apple slices, in the honey for a sweet year ahead. Please take time to explain the meaning of the special dishes and ritual to your children and guests.

A Dinner of Abundance

This dinner illustrates the role of food in relation to *Rosh Hashanah* 'best wishes'; it brings to your table an abundance of good things to eat as an omen for a plentiful year: fish, meat, a big selection of vegetables and special, sweet-smelling holiday baked goods. The menu offers a sample of all the traditional foods within the framework of a complete meal, yet guests will not feel stuffed if you serve small-to-medium portions.

The first course is Poached Fresh Carp. Prepare it a day ahead, so that the tasty stock can become a shimmering aspic. Serve the carp with fragrant, home-baked Round *Challah.* Chicken soup with very thin egg noodles may follow, but this course is optional, depending on the appetites of your family and guests.

The main course is a Pot of Plenty: pot-roasted meat with a harvest of vegetables. Start cooking it in the early afternoon to have it ready just in time for dinner. Don't worry about side dishes to accompany the meat, they are all in the 'pot of plenty'. Additional vegetables are served on the Fresh Vegetable Plate and dinner ends with *demitasse* or tea to accompany a very appropriate Honey Cake. The cake is served to signify a coming year that will be sweet as honey.

M E N U
(planned for 6 to 8)
Poached Fresh Carp*
Round Challah*
Chicken Soup with Egg-Noodles
Pot of Plenty—Pot Roast with Vegetables*
Fresh Vegetable Plate*
Honey Cake*
Demi-Tasse or Tea
Recipe given

POACHED FRESH CARP

Fresh carp, poached gently with aromatic vegetables, is a delicacy. It is good when served warm. It is even better when chilled thoroughly until the stock jells. For complete enjoyment eat the fish with *challah*, dipping pieces of it to soak up the stock on your plate.

    3 lb. fresh carp, sliced into serving portions
    3 large onions, sliced
    2 carrots, sliced
    2 celery stalks
    5 parsley sprigs
    2 tsp. salt
    ⅛ tsp. pepper
    1 tbls. sugar
    2 cups water

1. Put the vegetables, seasonings and the water in a large and shallow pot. Cover and let boil for 10 minutes.

2. Arrange the fish slices on the vegetables. Cover, reduce heat and simmer very gently for 1 hour. The carrots should be tender.

3. Taste the stock and correct seasoning. Remove fish carefully to a large platter. Strain the stock. Pour some over the fish and keep the remainder separately.

4. Serve warm, or refrigerate fish and reserved stock until the stock jells.

ROUND CHALLAH

Challah is a soft egg bread eaten on *Shabbat* and holidays. Generally it is braided, but on *Rosh Hashanah* the *challah* is round and shaped as a dome. The *challah* is beautifully brown on the outside with a rich yellow interior. When cut, the *challah* renders an honest-to-goodness aroma of homemade bread, and the raisins in it shine like little jewels.

For 2 Medium Round Challot

    1½ 0.6-oz. cakes fresh yeast
    ¼ cup warm water
    2/3 cup lukewarm water
    3 tbls. sugar
    1 tsp. salt
    3½-4 cups flour
    3 eggs at room temperature
    3 tbls. oil
    ¼ cup raisins
    1 egg yolk

1. Measure ¼ cup warm water and crumble the yeast into it. Let it rest for 3 minutes and stir to dissolve.

2. While the yeast is resting gather the other ingredients. Combine 3 cups flour with the salt in a large bowl. Make a well in the center.

3. When the yeast is dissolved add ½ cup flour and a pinch of sugar and blend well. Let rise for 10 minutes in a warm place. Pour the yeast mixture into the 'well' then add the sugar, eggs and the remaining lukewarm water.

4. Blend all ingredients with a big wooden spoon, or with your hand. Add the oil last. The dough may be quite sticky in the beginning so sprinkle in the remaining flour, little by little, and stir vigorously to make it manageable. Let rest for 3 minutes.

5. Turn the dough out on a lightly floured surface. If it is still sticky sprinkle with more flour, pick it up and slap it down on the surface. Repeat this act rapidly, scraping the dough off the surface with a spatula. In 2 to 3 minutes it should be moderately stiff and you can begin to knead.

6. To knead, flour your hands and pick up the edge of the dough at the point farthest from you. Fold over to the edge nearest you, and with the heel of your hand press down firmly, pushing the ball of dough away from you. Repeat 4 times and turn ¼ of a circle; repeat the folding and pressing, pushing and turning until the dough is smooth, satiny and elastic, about 5 to 8 minutes. Add the raisins, folding and kneading them in gently.

7. Clean the bowl, dry it and oil lightly. Put in the ball of dough and turn once to cover all over with oil. Cover the bowl with a clean towel and let stand in the kitchen, away from drafts, for 2 hours. Punch the dough down, kneading it again for 3 minutes and then let rise again for another hour.

8. Punch the dough down once more. Cut into 2 parts. Shape each into a 'rope', 20″ to 24″ long. Circle each 'rope' around itself so a round, dome-shaped *challah* is formed. *Preheat the oven to 350°F.*

9. Grease a large cookie sheet lightly. Put the 2 *challot* on it. Dilute the egg yolk in 2 table-spoons of tap water. Mix well and brush all over the *challot* with the mixture. Let them rest and rise for about 25 minutes.

10. Bake in a 350°F oven for about 50 minutes, until the *challot* reach a deep golden-brown color. If the tops brown too fast cover with aluminum foil for part of the baking.

11. Serve the *challot* whole. They are to be cut at the table after *Hamotzi* (Bread Benediction).

POT OF PLENTY—POT ROAST WITH PLENTY OF VEGETABLES

A truly gourmet dish that bursts with the flavor of the combined ingredients, and is relatively easy to execute. You may do the initial preparations as much as a day before dinner.

5 lb. shoulder of beef
2 tbls. flour
1/3 cup oil
1 large onion
3 cups beef stock
2 tsp. salt
⅛ tsp. pepper
2 celery stalks
1 bay leaf
2 garlic cloves
8 parsley sprigs
1 6-oz. can tomato paste

To be added later:
1 lb. carrots
1 lb. potatoes
1 lb. green beans
1 10-oz. pkg. frozen peas
1 10-oz. pkg. frozen cauliflower

1. Tie the meat so that it will keep its shape while cooking and sprinkle it all over with flour. Heat the oil in a big dutch-oven and brown the meat. This will take about 10 to 15 minutes, not less than 10, since the meat should be brown on all sides.

2. Slice the onion and add to the pot. Fry until golden. Pour off some of the fat.

3. Sprinkle with salt and pepper, and add 3 cups of beef stock (or water plus soup cubes). Add the celery, bay leaf, garlic, parsley, and tomato paste. Bring to a boil then cover, reduce the heat and simmer gently for 2 hours. *Cooking to this point can be done several hours or a day in advance.*

4. Clean and peel the carrots, potatoes and snip off the ends of the green beans. Arrange them in an organized way, around the meat. Taste and add salt if necessary. Let it simmer for another 50 minutes.

5. Discard the celery, bay leaf and parsley. Taste again. Add the frozen vegetables around the meat and cook for 7 minutes. Warm a big serving plate. Remove the meat from pot, discard the tying strings, cut off some of the excess fat.

6. Put the meat in the center of the serving plate and surround with the vegetables. Put the sauce through a sieve into a 2-quart saucepan. Boil briskly until reduced to about half (this takes approximately 10 minutes and makes the sauce thicker and richer). Keep warm.

7. Keep the platter warm on a food warmer or in a very slow oven (150°F), until serving time.

Just before you bring the platter to the table pour some sauce on the meat to make it look glossy. Put the remaining sauce in a nice sauceboat to pass separately. The meat surrounded by the vegetables makes a picture of abundance.

FRESH VEGETABLE PLATE

This plate will add color and beauty to the table and is a festive substitute for the usual tossed salad. You can refrigerate everything all day, except the tomatoes and dressing. Cover with aluminum foil.

6 lettuce leaves
3 medium tomatoes
2 cucumbers
6 radishes
6 small pickles
12 black olives

1. Clean the lettuce, tomatoes and radishes. Peel the cucumbers.

2. Slice tomatoes, make 'roses' from the radishes. Slice cucumbers.

3. Arrange the lettuce on a chilled plate and top with other vegetables, except the tomatoes.

4. Just before serving, place tomato slices on plate, then sprinkle with your favorite salad dressing or with salt, oil, and lemon juice. Serve immediately.

HONEY CAKE
(Photograph on page 8)

Honey cake is a special favorite anytime, but especially on *Rosh Hashanah*. The honey expresses a wish for a sweet year and also gives the cake delicate flavor and texture. The spices lend a delightful aroma and the whipped egg whites make it light. All in all—this cake is a winner.

4 eggs
¾ cup sugar
1 cup honey (12 oz.)
1/3 cup salad oil
3 cups flour
½ tsp. salt
2 tsp. baking powder
1 tsp. baking soda
½ tsp. ground clove
½ tsp. ground allspice
3 tsp. instant coffee
1 cup hot water

1. Preheat the oven to 325°F. Set out a baking pan with a 7-cup capacity (7¼″ x 7¼″ x 2″). Grease lightly and set aside. Prepare a strong cup of coffee with the hot water and instant coffee. Cool.

2. Separate the eggs. Put the yolks in a big mixing bowl, and the whites in a medium one. Beat the yolks with the sugar until creamy. Add the oil then the honey—beating after each addition. Beat until the mixture is smooth and creamy.

3. Sift the flour and measure 3 cups. Combine with salt, baking powder, baking soda and spices.

4. Add the dry ingredients to the egg-honey mixture alternately with the coffee, stirring with a spatula or a wooden spoon. Stir only until all ingredients are well blended. Do not overmix.

5. Clean and dry the beaters. Whip the egg whites until stiff and can hold their shape. Add, one-third at a time, to the batter. Fold in gently, until the batter is smooth.

6. Pour into the greased pan and bake in the preheated oven for about 80 to 90 minutes. The cake is done when a toothpick comes out dry and clean.

7. This cake keeps well. In fact, it improves with a little aging. So bake several days ahead. This will allow the cake to acquire full flavor and typical texture.

A Dinner of Robust Flavors

Keynote for this dinner is robust flavor along with traditional foods. The fish is baked in a piquant tomato sauce, inspired by Jewish-*Sephardic* cookery. The main course is Roast Duckling, accented by a touch of garlic for new, added zest. It is served with a Golden Carrot *Tzimmes,* delicately seasoned with cinnamon, that represents the Jewish-*Ashkenazi* way of cooking. Included also are Whole Roast Potatoes, cooked in the same oven as the duckling. The Clear Chicken Soup is flavorful and hot. It can be prepared ahead and served with store-bought soup-almonds. This meal ends with a magnificent Apple and Honey Strudel and tea.

MENU
(planned for 6 to 8)
Baked Fish in Tomato Sauce*
Clear Chicken Soup*
Roast Duckling*
Whole Roast Potatoes*
Golden Carrot Tzimmes*
Small Green Salad
Apple and Honey Strudel*
Tea

**Recipe given*

BAKED FISH IN TOMATO SAUCE

Tomato sauce and herbs give the fish a piquant flavor that is just right for a first course. Being baked in one piece the fish looks beautiful on a serving platter.

    2 lb. fish (one large or two small)
    2 tsp. salt
    ⅛ tsp. pepper
    1 large onion
    4 tbls. oil
    6 parsley sprigs, chopped
    1 6-oz. can of tomato sauce
    1 tsp. garlic powder
    Juice of one lemon
    1 cup water

1. Grease a baking dish with a little oil.

2. Slice the onion and fry it lightly in a skillet with the rest of the oil.

3. Combine the tomato sauce with the parsley and garlic.

4. Clean the fish, sprinkle with salt and pepper, and arrange in the baking dish. Top with the fried onions and with the oil. Cover with seasoned tomato sauce. (If too thick, dilute it with a little water).

5. Combine the water with the lemon juice and pour around the fish. Bake, covered, in a 400°F oven for 30 minutes. Remove the cover and bake another 20 minutes at 350°F.

6. Lift carefully onto a serving platter. Garnish with additional parsely sprigs and slices of lemon.

CLEAR CHICKEN SOUP

Fresh aromatic vegetables are the secret of a good chicken soup. Celery root releases so much flavor, as do the carrots, Italian squash and onions. Be sure to use them.

2 lb. chicken wings and giblets, except livers
1 lb. beef shin bones
4 carrots
1 large onion
½ celery root, or 3 celery stalks
1 parsnip
10 parsley sprigs
2 Italian squash (Zucchini)
⅛ tsp. pepper
1 tbls. salt
10 cups water

1. Clean the chicken and beef bones, put them in a large soup pot.

2. Clean and pare the vegetables. Add to the pot with the water and seasonings. Bring to a boil, then lower the heat.

3. Skim off the foam with a slotted spoon. Cover and let the soup simmer gently for 1½ to 2 hours.

4. Taste. Add more salt and pepper if needed. When the soup is done, take out the meat, bones and vegetables. Pour broth through a sieve or colander so you will have clear soup.

5. Serve with soup almonds.

ROAST DUCKLING

A light touch of garlic adds zest to the duckling, and slow roasting makes it brown and crisp. Prepare two birds for eight people since a duckling is not a meaty bird.

2 4 to 5 lb. ducklings
Seasoned salt
Pepper
Garlic powder

1. Sprinkle the ducklings generously with the seasoned salt, pepper and garlic powder. (Or mash 3 cloves of fresh garlic and use them instead.) Rub the seasonings well into the skin and the insides of the birds.

2. Truss each duckling so it will have a nice shape when done, and place side by side, breast up, on a rack in a shallow pan. Roast, uncovered, at 375°F oven for 1 hour; turn and brown on the other side for another hour. (Ducklings have much fat under their skin and there is no need for basting.) After an hour of baking prick the ducklings' skin with a fork to allow more fat to drip. This makes them crisper.

3. If you prepare Whole Roast Potatoes (next

recipe), put the potatoes in the oven about 1 hour before the ducklings are done. You can add them to the roasting pan, or, if the pan is too small transfer the fat and juice to another pan, and roast the potatoes in it.

4. When the ducklings are done take out of the oven, discard trussing threads and place on a warm platter. Bring to the table whole to show your guests the nice, brown ducklings. We recommend, however, that you do the carving on a side table or in the kitchen. (Kitchen-scissors are very handy for doing the job.)

WHOLE ROAST POTATOES

Boiling the potatoes briefly before roasting gives them an interesting texture and flavor.

2 lb. small potatoes (8 potatoes)

1. Peel and boil the potatoes in salted water until just tender—about 10 minutes. (You can do it several hours before dinner time.)

2. Add potatoes to the duckling pan about 1 hour before the ducklings are done. Turn potatoes occasionally to brown evenly on all sides.

GOLDEN CARROT TZIMMES

Carrot *Tzimmes* is a sweet and flavorful concoction of carrots, prunes, raisins, nuts, honey and cinnamon. It is served with the main dish, meat or chicken, and is the 'Jewish Style' equivalent to spiced apples side-dish in other cookery.

1½ lb. carrots
3 tbls. margarine
½ tsp. salt
1 cup water
½ cup raisins
1 cup prunes
6 tbls. brown sugar
½ tsp. cinnamon
¼ tsp. ground cloves
1 tbls. lemon juice
2 tbls. chopped candied orange peel
2 tbls. honey

1. Peel the carrots and slice into ⅛″ thick slices. Melt the margarine in a medium large saucepan. Add the carrots and sauté for about 5 minutes. Add the water and sugar and bring to a boil.

2. Stir in remaining ingredients and lower the heat. Cover and let simmer over low heat for 2 hours. Check occasionally to see if it simmers, and if there is enough fluid.

3. Remove the cover at the end of 2 hours and cook for 20 minutes longer. The *tzimmes* should be moist but not too soupy. Serve hot.

APPLE AND HONEY STRUDEL
(Photograph on page 8)

Strudel is a mouth-watering, rolled-up cake filled with a variety of fruits. The filling is tender and moist, while the crust around it is crisp and flaky. Our Strudel is filled with apples, raisins and honey, traditional elements of *Rosh Hashanah*. It is sprinkled with confectioners' sugar and is as lovely to look at as it is good to eat.

For 2 Strudels, 15″ Long

Pastry:
2½ cups flour
8 oz. margarine (2 sticks)
½ cup cold water
1 tsp. vinegar
¼ tsp. salt

Apple filling:
4 tart medium-sized apples
2 tbls. sugar
2 tbls. honey
½ cup raisins
½ cup pulverized almonds
1 tsp. cinnamon
4 tbls. bread crumbs

For assembling:
2 tbls. oil
2 tbls. bread crumbs
1 small egg
2 tbls. water
¼ cup confectioners' sugar

1. Measure the flour into a big bowl. Use a pastry blender or 2 knives to cut the margarine into the flour until the mixture resembles small peas. Now work with your fingertips crumbling the margarine in the flour until it resembles cornmeal.

2. Combine in a measuring cup the water, vinegar and salt, and drizzle it over the flour. Blend with a fork then knead with your hand 40 kneads. The dough is quite soft at the beginning, but will become elastic as you go along. Complete

the kneading by taking the whole dough in your hand and slamming it against the bowl. Pick up the dough and slam it 20 times. At the end the dough will be very elastic and manageable. (You may do the slamming on the work table or other surface, lined with wax paper to save on cleaning.) After the kneading and slamming, which takes only about 5 minutes, shape dough into 2 balls. Wrap them with waxed paper and let rest in the refrigerator for 1 hour.

3. When you start the final assembly and baking of the Strudels—preheat the oven to 375°F. Remove the dough from the refrigerator to roll it out. Dust your working surface with flour and roll out a rectangle, out of each ball, of about 12″ x 15″ (approximately the size of a cookie sheet or a jelly-roll pan).

4. Prepare the filling: Peel the apples and grate them on a coarse grater. Add all other filling ingredients and mix well.

5. Brush each rectangle with 1 tablespoon oil and sprinkle all over with half of the bread crumbs. Divide the filling into 2 equal parts, using 1 part for each. With a tablespoon put mounds of the filling on the dough in a lengthwise strip, about 3″ wide. For easier rolling, put the filling-strip 1″ away from the long edge. 'Iron' the filling with the back of a tablespoon to make it smooth and even. Roll up lengthwise, starting by folding the 1″ edge over the filling, then rolling like a jelly roll. Repeat the same with the second dough rectangle and the other half of the filling.

6. Transfer the strudels to a cookie sheet or a jelly roll pan very carefully. Place on pan with the smooth side up and the fold underneath. Pinch the open edges and tuck under themselves.

7. Beat the egg and water together well then brush on tops of the strudels. To prevent strudels bursting while baking make 1″ diagonal cuts in the tops, spacing them about 1″ apart, with a sharp knife.

8. Bake in a 375°F oven for 1 hour, or until the strudels are nicely browned. Cool and sprinkle with confectioners' sugar.

II
YOM KIPPUR:
A SOLEMN FESTIVITY

ACCORDING TO JEWISH TRADITION, God's judgment of man and his fate for the coming year is made on *Rosh Hashanah*; the final verdict is given on the Holy Day of Atonement, *Yom Kippur*. Therefore, the period between the two holidays is devoted to prayers, charity, repentance and examination of one's thoughts and deeds. This is done in the hope of receiving a positive verdict. While the greetings exchanged on *Rosh Hashanah* express general wishes for a Happy New Year, those for *Yom Kippur* are more specific. During this holiday the wish is 'may your final verdict be favorable.'

The Day of Atonement is a day of fasting. Usually, Jews do not eat a bite of food or drink one sip of water; they dress in white and spend the entire day in the Synagogue. Fasting is undertaken as proof that one can abstain for one day from temptations and pleasure. In so doing the meaning of confessions and prayers is deepened.

At sunset, the day of fasting and prayer ends with the sounding of the *Shofar,* (ram's horn). Now, light refreshments are taken: perhaps a cup of tea and a delicate sweet. A little later, dinner that suits the personal preferences of each family is enjoyed. Some like salty foods, such as herring, to compensate for the loss of body salts; others prefer dairy dishes.

After a solemn beginning the Day of Atonement closes with its celebrants strengthened in character and filled with confidence. Initial preparations for the next joyous holiday, *Succot,* begin that same evening.

A Satisfying Dinner Before the Fast

On *Erev Yom Kippur,* the eve of the Day of Atonement, lunch is a full meal, designed to ease the period of fasting that is to come. It is followed by a festal dinner, served before sunset, that resembles the elaborate eating on the eve of *Rosh Hashanah. Challah* (home-baked white bread) is put on the table and the white holiday candles are lit by mother. The mood is solemn and the meal well-balanced without being heavy. Over-eating makes the fast unpleasant. There are no fried foods and no very sweet or

The festive and solemn setting fits the spirit of Yom Kippur, the Jewish High Holy Day. The GOLDEN CHICKEN SOUP (recipe on page 19), and the KREPLACH (recipe on page 20) are eaten in the festive meal before the fast begins.

spicy dishes. Fruit juice and a cooked fruit dessert are served instead. This is to avoid thirst as much as possible and to make digestion easier.

On our menu we have Fish Steamed in its own Juices, Golden Chicken Soup with *Kreplach* (little dough 'pockets' filled with meat), that are a traditional *Yom Kippur* dish, Simmered Chicken accompanied by Fluffy Potato Purée and Mixed Colorful Vegetables. A simple salad may be added. At the end, a good, homemade Fruit Compote followed by Carrot Torte will be very satisfying. The whole menu is planned for four to six persons, since this meal is eaten generally in the intimacy of the immediate family.

M E N U
(planned for 4 to 6)
Fish Steamed in its own Juices*
Golden Chicken Soup*
Kreplach*
Simmered Chicken*
Fluffy Potato Purée*
Mixed Colorful Vegetables
Sliced Tomatoes
Fruit Compote*
Carrot Torte*
Tea or Demi-Tasse
Recipe given

FISH STEAMED IN ITS OWN JUICES

The fish cooks gently in a covered dish and comes out flaky and delicate. Use the natural pan juices as your sauce.

> 1 lb. fish filets
> 3 tbls margarine
> 2 tbls. lemon juice
> 1 tbls. finely chopped onion
> ½ tsp. salt

1. Clean the fish, and cut into serving portions if necessary. Sprinkle with salt on both sides.

2. Grease a medium baking dish and arrange the fish in it. Sprinkle the fish with lemon juice and with chopped onion.

3. Cut the margarine into small pieces and dot the fish. Or melt the margarine and pour over fish.

4. Cover the dish and put in a 350°F oven for 25 minutes until the fish flakes easily with a fork.

SIMMERED CHICKEN and GOLDEN CHICKEN SOUP
(Photograph on page 18)

Plump chicken, simmered in rich broth with fresh vegetables, creates two delicacies: golden soup in which to serve the *kreplach* and a main course of juicy, tender chicken. The soup becomes stronger and better because of the whole chicken cooked in it, while the chicken itself absorbs all the goodness of its cooking companions.

> 2 plump 3-lb. chickens
> 8 cups water
> 1 big onion
> 3 carrots
> 3 celery stalks
> 1 tbls. salt
> 10 parsley sprigs

[19]

1. Clean the chickens and cut them into quarters (or have the butcher do it for you). Clean the giblets thoroughly. Clean the vegetables too; peel and quarter the carrots and onions.

2. Put the water, chickens, giblets (except liver), vegetables and salt in a large deep pot. Bring to a boil then lower the heat and simmer, covered, for 2 hours or until the chicken is fork-tender. Check occasionally and add water if too much evaporates.

3. Cool the chicken in the soup. Later, transfer the chicken portions to a serving plate. Skim some of the fat from the soup, and strain through a sieve into a large bowl. Use immediately or store in refrigerator until needed. Reheat before serving.

KREPLACH
(Photograph on page 18)

Kreplach, traditional favorites for *Yom Kippur,* are little dough 'pockets' full of goodness that are delicious when served in hot chicken soup. Serve two or three to a soup bowl. The rest can be refrigerated or frozen for later use.

For 20 Kreplach

Dough:
2 cups flour
2 egg yolks
½ tsp. salt
½ cup water

Meat filling:
1 cup ground, cooked beef or chicken
1 egg
1 big onion
1 tbls. bread crumbs
2 tbls. salad oil
1 tsp. salt
Dash of pepper
3 tsp. instant chicken bouillon powder

1. When cooking a soup, reserve some pieces of meat. They may be parts of the chicken breast, giblets, etc. Grind the meat in a grinder, a blender, or chop very finely with a knife.

2. Dice the onion and fry in the oil until golden brown. Add the ground meat and cook together for 5 minutes. Remove from heat, cool and add the egg, pepper, salt, 1 teaspoon of the bouillon powder and the bread crumbs, and mix well.

3. Sift the flour and salt into a large bowl. Mix

the yolks and water, then add to the flour. Work in flour until a dough forms. Knead with your hands, at least 40 kneads, until the dough is smooth and elastic.

4. Roll out the dough on a floured surface. For light and tasteful *kreplach,* the dough should be rolled out as thin as possible. Cut into 3" squares. Put a teaspoonful of filling in the center of each square. Fold over to form a triangle. Moisten the edges and pinch them together to seal tightly.

5. Put a triangle you just made on the table, with the fold towards you. Lift the two side corners with your hands, and attach them to each other with a pinch.

6. Boil 10 cups of water with the remaining 2 teaspoons chicken bouillon powder in a big pot. Drop in the *kreplach* and boil for about 15 minutes. *Kreplach* are done when they float on top of the liquid. Take them out carefully with a slotted spoon. Drain well. Serve hot in soup.

FLUFFY POTATO PUREE

Enjoy this fluffy side dish with the chicken. For maximum taste, it is important that the potatoes be cooked and puréed at the last minute.

2 lb. russet or white potatoes
2 oz. margarine (½ stick)
½ cup very hot chicken soup
1 tbls. snipped parsley
1 tsp. salt

1. Peel potatoes and cut into small cubes. If you want to do this job ahead, put cubes in water; they will keep for several hours.

2. Before serving time, drain the cubed potatoes and place in a medium pot. Cover with water, add salt and cook for 10 to 15 minutes. Drain and return to heat for 1 or 2 minutes, shaking the pot gently to dry the potatoes.

3. Mash the potatoes with an electric mixer or a potato-masher. Add the hot soup and margarine gradually, beating continuously until the potatoes are fluffy. This can be made just before dinner time. To keep warm, cover the pot and set in a pan of very hot water.

4. Bring the puréed potatoes to the table in a serving dish, sprinkled with snipped parsley.

FRUIT COMPOTE

Marvelous end to a rich meal, fruit compote is a perfect choice for *Yom Kippur*. Once a treat reserved only for holiday and *Shabbat,* it can be prepared a day ahead which makes it even more attractive at a busy time.

    1½ lb. mixed dried fruit
    6 cups water
    2 tbls. lemon juice
    ½ cup sugar

1. Soak the dry fruit in the water for 2 hours.

2. Bring to a boil in soaking liquid. Add sugar and lemon juice, lower the heat and cover the pot. Cook for about 45 minutes, or until tender. Chill and serve cold.

CARROT TORTE

The unique combination of carrots and almonds makes this torte a moist and flaky treat. A lacing of Orange Liqueur turns this holiday specialty into a special delight.

    1 lb. carrots
    6 eggs
    1½ cups sugar
    1 tsp. grated orange rind
    1 tsp. orange liqueur
    1½ cups ground almonds (6 oz.)
    ½ cup flour
    1 tsp. baking powder

1. Peel the carrots, slice and cook in 1 cup water until tender, about 15 minutes. Drain them and push through a sieve or mash in an electric blender.

2. Beat the egg yolks in a bowl. Add the sugar, beating until thick and light in color. Stir in the carrots, orange rind, liqueur, ground almonds, flour and baking powder. Mix lightly.

3. Preheat the oven to 325°F. Grease a 9″ springform pan.

4. Beat the egg whites until stiff but not dry. Fold ¼ into the carrot mixture. Add another ¼, then fold this into the remainder of the whites. Fold very carefully but thoroughly.

5. Bake for 50 minutes, or until a tooth pick comes out clean.

6. Cool and take out of the springform. This cake keeps well and moist when completely wrapped with saran or aluminum foil, in the refrigerator.

In the center of the picture is a plate with STUFFED CAB-
BAGE (recipe on page 25). The tall silver container in the
back holds an Etrog, an Israeli citrus fruit. In the front is a
Shofar (ram's horn). Both are used during the High Holiday season.

III

SUCCOT: GIVING THANKS WARMLY IN AUTUMN

SUCCOT IS A HAPPY HOLIDAY on the Jewish calendar. Literally, *Succot* means 'Booths'. The holiday commemorates the journey from slavery in ancient Egypt to freedom in the Land of Israel that was made some four-thousand years ago by the Jewish ancestors. They wandered in the desert for forty years, living in temporary booths, and for generations now it has been the custom to build a *Succah*, 'booth', outside the house: in the yard or on a balcony.

The walls of a *Succah* are made with sheets and rugs; palm branches serve as the roof to let the stars peek through at night. The booth is big enough to accommodate a table, so that the family may eat its meals in the *Succah* during the seven days of the holiday. Adults and children collaborate in erecting the *Succah* and trimming it with pictures, handicrafts, flowers and fruits. Everyone enjoys building the *Succah* and use it as often as possible: sitting and talking, eating, singing and entertaining friends. All of these activities help to remind them again and again of the transition from slavery to freedom.

Succot coincides with the end of the fruit harvest period. In ancient Israel farmers went on pilgrimage to Jerusalem during this holiday to bring gifts of their crops to the Temple. Through the centuries Jews, far from their Promised Land, have celebrated seven days of *Succot* to mark the happy harvest and thanksgiving days of their fore-fathers. A bountiful harvest is represented by the fresh fruits and flowers that adorn the *Succah* as well as by the abundance of vegetables and fruits in the meals.

Simhat Torah is celebrated on the eighth day of *Succot*. The name means 'being happy with the *Torah*' and indicates the merry spirit of this holiday. On *Simhat Torah* a full year of reciting the *Torah* in the synagogue comes to an end and a new one begins. This has always been a source of great happiness and the holiday differs from most others in its jollity. Most of the festivity occurs in the Synagogue. The scrolls of *Torah* are taken out of their usual place and carried around, the *Hakafot,* while people sing and dance with them. The children join the fun, singing and dancing with their fathers and waving little flags decorated with apples and candles.

[23]

A Family Supper for a Chilly Evening

The main attraction of this holiday is its unusual setting: the *Succah*, a booth built and decorated solely for this holiday. Since the air is somewhat chilly and crisp at this time of year our menu is planned around dishes that will reach the table while still hot. We recommend that you bring the food in big, covered serving dishes from the kitchen; if brought in individual plates, the food cools too quickly.

The menu reflects the fact that it is harvest time, starting with delicious, satisfying Old-Fashioned Barley Soup. The main course is a traditional specialty for *Succot*: Stuffed Cabbage. Colorful, with the green of the cabbage surrounded by the deep red of the spicy tomato sauce, this piquant main course finds its ideal companion in Perfect Steamed Rice, cooked so each grain keeps to itself without sticking to the others. We suggest serving the salad, European style, as a side dish. A marvelous Apple Meringue Torte ends dinner. (The torte is equally good when served hot, directly from the oven, or cold.)

MENU
(planned for 4 to 6)
Old-Fashioned Barley Soup*
Stuffed Cabbage*
Perfect Steamed Rice*
Mixed Vegetable Salad*
Apple Meringue Torte*
Black Coffee or Tea
Recipe given

OLD-FASHIONED BARLEY SOUP

This old-fashioned barley soup brings back memories of good old days when soup, simmering slowly on the stove, filled the house with wonderful smells. The soup is easy to make and can be prepared in advance to be reheated·when needed. Thick and satisfying, it will keep warm in the *Succah.*

```
1 lb. chicken wings and giblets except livers
1 cup diced carrots
1 cup diced celery
1 tbls. onion flakes
1 tbls. parsley flakes
1 beef bouillon cube
1/3 cup barley
2 tsp. salt
⅛ tsp. pepper
8 cups water
```

1. Clean the wings and giblets and put them in a soup pot. You could also use other parts of the chicken, but this soup is a good way to utilize the giblets when you wish to broil or roast the meatier parts.

2. Dice and measure the carrots and celery and add to the pot. Other vegetables such as squash and potatoes may be used as well. Add the flakes of onion and parsley (or use fresh parsley and one medium onion).

3. Add seasonings and barley. Bring to a boil, reduce heat and just let simmer an hour. The soup should be creamy and the barley tender. Add water if necessary and correct seasoning.

STUFFED CABBAGE
(Photograph on page 22)

A traditional specialty for *Succot.* The leaves of the cabbage are stuffed with savory ground meat, rolled up and cooked in tomato sauce. This dish has a pleasant sweet-tart taste.

```
1 head cabbage
2 tbls. oil
1 large onion, chopped
1 lb. ground beef
1 egg
½ cup bread crumbs
1 garlic clove, mashed
1 tsp. salt
⅛ tsp. pepper
2 cups tomato juice
1 tsp. beef bouillon powder
2 tbls. sugar
Juice from one lemon
```

1. Lower the cabbage into a big pot of boiling water. Turn off the heat, cover, and let soak while you prepare the filling.

2. Fry the chopped onion in the oil until just golden yellow. Add to the ground meat with the egg, bread crumbs, mashed garlic, salt and pepper. Mix well.

3. Lift the cabbage out of the hot water, drain and separate carefully. The leaves separate easily and are manageable. Put them on a big flat plate.

4. Grease a big saucepan. Put a little filling on each leaf and fold it like an envelope or roll it so that the filling will not spill out. Put the stuffed leaves, very close together, in the saucepan, folded side down.

5. Combine the tomato juice with the beef bouillon powder, add the sugar and lemon juice. Pour over the stuffed cabbage and cook, covered, for about an hour on moderate heat.

PERFECT STEAMED RICE

The proof of a well prepared rice is not only in the eating but in its appearance. A perfect rice dish should allow each grain to be distinctly separated from each other. To accomplish this, the rice is fried gently and then steamed to perfection.

```
1 cup long grain rice
3 tbls. oil
1 medium onion, chopped
2 cups water
1 tsp. salt
1 beef bouillon cube
```

1. In a medium saucepan fry the chopped onion until just golden. Add the rice and fry it, stirring continuously, for about 3 minutes, until the rice is ivory white. Immediately add the water, salt, and bouillon cube.

2. Bring to a quick boil. Let boil briskly for 3 minutes then reduce the heat to the lowest point. When the boiling subsides cover the pan tightly and continue cooking on the lowest heat for 25 minutes without stirring or opening the pan. Turn off the heat.

3. Leave the rice in the covered pan until serving time then fluff it up with 2 forks and serve it piping hot.

MIXED VEGETABLE SALAD

Be sure to include some fresh vegetable on your *Succot* menu. This perky one will add color and a crisp texture contrast.

1 small head of lettuce
2 tomatoes
1 cucumber
1 bell pepper
2 shredded carrots
2 tbls. olive or salad oil
Juice from one lemon
Salt, pepper, dash of sugar

1. Cut the vegetables into bite-size chunks.

2. Just prior to serving season to taste with the oil, lemon juice, salt, pepper and a dash of sugar.

APPLE MERINGUE TORTE

Simple but deliciously impressive, this apple meringue torte is composed of three layers. The bottom is crusty and bursts with the flavor of the added egg yolks. The second layer is made of grated apples flavored with cinnamon. And on the top are peaks of white and gold meringue. You can prepare the bottom layer ahead of time and add the rest before baking.

Crust:
6 oz. margarine (1½ sticks)
3 egg yolks
¾ cup sugar
2¼ cups flour
½ tsp. vanilla extract
½ tsp. baking powder

Apple filling:
2 big, tart apples
1 tsp. cinnamon
1 tbls. flour

Meringue topping:
3 egg whites
½ cup sugar

1. Grease and flour a 9″ springform. Preheat the oven to 350°F.

2. Cream the margarine, vanilla and egg yolks until fluffy. Add the dry ingredients and stir well with a wooden spoon. If mixture seems dry add 2 tablespoons water. Shape dough into a ball.

3. Dip your hands in flour and flatten the ball in the springform. Build a 'wall' of dough around the edge.

4. Bake for about 20 minutes or until the crust is golden.

5. Grate the apples on a coarse grater. Add the flour and cinnamon. Mix well then spread on the crust.

6. Beat the egg whites, adding the sugar gradually, until stiff peaks form and all the sugar dissolves. Spread over apple layer.

7. Bake in a slow oven (250°F) for about 25 minutes until the meringue is browned to a nice golden color.

IV
HANUKKAH: HEARTY PARTIES ON WINTRY NIGHTS

Hanukkah, which usually takes place near the end of December, is known as the Festival of Lights. It is an eight-day holiday celebrated by candle lighting, eating *latkes* (potato pancakes), singing and having fun.

A typical *Hanukkah* evening consists of family and friends coming together to light the candles and sing *Hanukkah* songs. After that children receive presents—sometimes even money, called *Hanukkah Gelt*, that may be real or made of chocolate. Then, hot holiday specialties are served to delight everyone; while adults converse the youngsters spin the *dreidel* (top), betting their recently received money on the side that will be up when the *dreidel* topples.

The name of the holiday refers to the ceremony of sanctifying the Temple in ancient Jerusalem twenty-one centuries ago. At that time the huge armies of the Greek Empire were defeated by the brave Yehudah Hamaccabee and a small band of supporters. The Greeks were driven out of Jerusalem and the Temple was then cleansed of all foreign elements. The *Menorah* in the Temple was relighted with pure oil. According to tradition, only a very small jug of oil, enough for one day, could be found, yet it lasted for eight days, which was considered a miracle. Since then, *Hanukkah* has been celebrated for eight days. On the long, wintry nights of the holiday stories are told of Jewish heroism that dates back centuries and the never forgotten miracles.

Hanukkah's traditional foods are related to the oil miracle by being fried in oil. Their variety is big and delicious with *latkes, pontchekes* and doughnuts leading the popularity list. (Recipes for all of these are given in this chapter.)

Hanukkah is the perfect holiday for friendly entertaining and the traditional fried specialties of the season lend themselves to winter parties.

Planning Successful Parties

As hostess you can have fun at your own parties by careful planning and do-ahead preparation. A good menu is a great help, of course, and you will find three complete menus here for the family alone or family and guests.

The first menu is a buffet supper that features traditional favorites brought up-to-date. The supper is hot, hearty and easily managed. The second menu 'says cheese' with a welcoming smile, while the third provides a variety of meat snacks.

A word of advice. When you serve snacks and canapés, pick those that can be prepared ahead of time and serve only two or three homemade goodies. Purchase the others. Guests always prefer a smiling hostess to a wealth of homemade *hor d'oeuvres*.

Hanukkah Specialties

TRADITIONAL LATKES

Latkes are potato pancakes which taste ever so delicious on *Hanukkah*. They are brown, crisp and heart-warming. You may serve them with sour cream or apple sauce but be sure to enjoy them with friends and *mishpoche* (relatives), because 'togetherness' is what *Hanukkah* is all about.

For 20 Latkes

2 lb. potatoes
2 eggs
1 tsp. salt
2 tbls. flour or matzo meal
¼ tsp. baking powder
1 small onion
1 small apple
Oil for frying
Sour cream
Apple sauce

1. Peel and grate the potatoes on a coarse grater and drain. Peel and grate the onion and the apple.

2. Beat the eggs lightly in a medium bowl. Add the grated potatoes, onion and apple and blend weli. Add salt, flour and baking powder. Mix thoroughly.

3. Pour about 1″ of oil into a large skillet and heat. Drop the pancake mixture by tablespoons into the hot oil. Fry and brown on both sides.

4. Serve the *latkes* hot. Accompany them with bowls of sour cream and apple sauce.

Note: You can use an electric blender for grating. Cut each potato into 8 pieces, put in the blender and cover with water. Close the lid and blend at medium speed for 5 seconds. Drain completely through a mesh sieve. Put potatoes into a bowl and proceed immediately.

THE HANUKKAH 'MIRACLES'

Since oil is such an important element in the *Hanukkah* story, it is used in many of the typical dishes. Here is a recipe for a small 'miracle': little fried-flour-and-eggs cakes that are crisp and delicious. They will be enjoyed tremendously on the happy *Hanukkah* evenings.

For 30-40 Pieces

1½ cups flour
2 eggs
2 tbls. milk
½ tsp. salt
Oil for frying
Confectioners' sugar

1. Measure the flour and salt into a bowl. Beat the eggs with the milk in a separate bowl then combine with flour. Work with your fingers to form a soft, smooth dough. If needed, add a little more flour.

2. Divide the dough into 2 balls. Roll out each ball in a very thin round on a well floured surface then stretch it with your fingers to make it even thinner. The thinner the dough, the better the 'miracles'.

3. Cut the dough into 2″ squares. Make an incision with a sharp knife in the middle of each square. Pull one end of the square through the incision so it looks like a knot.

4. Heat 1″ of oil in a large skillet.

5. Fry the 'knots' in the hot oil about 8 at a time. Turn so they become golden brown on both sides. Take out of the oil and drain on paper towels. Sprinkle with confectioners' sugar.

QUICK DOUGHNUTS

Eating doughnuts is one of the favorite customs of *Hanukkah*. Usually they are made of yeast dough, but here is a quick new way to prepare them: instead of waiting for the yeast dough to rise, use baking-powder-dough.

For More Than a Dozen

2 eggs
½ cup sugar
¼ cup oil
2¼ cups flour
2 tsp. baking powder
¼ tsp. salt
½ tsp. vanilla extract
½ tsp. grated lemon rind
Oil for deep frying
Sugar for sprinkling

1. Beat eggs and sugar thoroughly for 3 minutes with an electric mixer; add milk, oil and mix well.

2. Combine the flour, baking powder and salt. Add to eggs. Stir with a wooden spoon but do not overmix. The dough should be smooth and soft.

You should be able to manage it with hands dipped in flour.

3. Roll the dough ½″ thick on a lightly floured surface or flatten with your hands to same thickness.

4. To cut out, use a doughnut cutter or the old stand-by team of a water glass for the outside and a thimble to make the center hole. Dip the cutting tools in flour before using.

5. Heat 1½″ oil in a big, heavy skillet. Drop in doughnuts and fry until brown. Turn once. Drain on paper towels then sprinkle with sugar.

A Hot Buffet Supper

(Photograph on page 30)

The eight nights of *Hanukkah* may be cold and gray outside, but you can have it warm and cozy inside with an informal atmosphere and a hot buffet supper. Our menu is composed of fix-ahead dishes, some with a modern 'twist' and all easy to serve. When they are assembled on the buffet table, they make a lovely picture that invites your guests to help themselves.

The table setting is casual and colorful: ceramic casserole, wooden salad bowl and enamelled warmers. *Hanukkah* candles cast a warm glow and add beauty. (Use the picture as your guide for choosing serving bowls and arranging the table.)

The buffet features hot *hors d'oeuvres* that fit the *Hanukkah* mood, but are actually quite modern: *latkes* (potato pancakes). The main dish is a full meal in a casserole, Gourmet Meat Cooked in Wine and Vegetables. To add fresh garden flavor to the meal, prepare a nicely dressed salad, plus a tray with pickles and olives. The dessert, while characteristic of *Hanukkah,* is new and interesting: *Pontchekes* (doughnuts shaped like balls), served fondue style with Dessert Sauces for dipping.

The most appropriate beverage for this suppper is hot, sweet, black tea. Once tea is served you are all set to bring out the *dreidels* and some *Hanukkah Gelt.* Enjoy. Enjoy.

MENU
(planned for 6 to 8)

Modern Potato Latkes*
Gourmet Meat Cooked in Wine*
Salad
Relishes
Paradise Pontchekes*
with Dessert Sauces:
Chocolate Sauce*
Orange Sauce*
Tea

*Recipe given

HOT BUFFET SUPPER FOR HANUKKAH. At the center is MEAT COOKED IN WINE (recipe on page 31). In front are MODERN POTATO LATKES (recipe on page 31). In back are PARADISE PONTCHEKES (recipe on page 31), and in front of them, in enameled heaters are CHOCOLATE SAUCE (recipe on page 32) and ORANGE SAUCE (recipe on page 32). On the right, in the background, is a Hanukkiah, the special candelabra used during Hanukkah (known also as Menorah) to light the colorful candles.

MODERN POTATO LATKES
(Photograph on page 30)

We bring a traditional *Hanukkah* specialty up-to-date by using instant mashed potatoes to save time. Then we appeal to the diet-conscious by baking these *latkes* instead of frying them.

For 16 to 20 Latkes

1 cup mashed potatoes
2 oz. margarine (½ stick)
½ cup flour
2 eggs
½ tsp. salt
Dash white pepper
1 tsp. dehydrated onion flakes

1. Preheat the oven to 400°F.

2. Prepare the mashed potatoes according to package directions *substituting water for milk.* (Or, boil and mash ½ pound fresh potatoes.) Add the margarine, flour, eggs, seasonings and onion flakes. Mix well after each addition.

3. Fill a big pastry bag fitted with a ½" round tip with the potato mixture. Press out *latkes* on a lightly greased cookie sheet to resemble a lady-finger 3" long.

4. Reduce the oven temperature to 375°F, and bake the *latkes* for about 15 minutes. They should puff a little and have a golden color. Serve immediately.

Note: You may prepare the potato mixture several hours before serving time, then shape and bake them at the last moment.

GOURMET MEAT COOKED IN WINE
(Photograph on page 30)

This main dish contains meat cooked in wine and vegetables. Please note two innovations: we omit the potatoes, and add chickpeas for more interesting flavor and texture.

4 lb. roasting beef
Oil for frying
½ cup flour
½ cup diced onions
4 carrots, diced
2 cloves garlic
1 8-oz. can tomato sauce
Salt, pepper and bay leaf
1 cup red wine
18 small white onions, peeled
18 small mushrooms, whole
1 1-lb. can chickpeas (garbanzo beans)

1. Cut the meat into small chunks and dip in flour. Fry them in the oil until brown all over. Remove to a casserole with a tight-fitting lid.

2. Fry the onions and carrots in the same oil. Transfer to casserole.

3. Put the remaining ingredients, except the last 3, in the casserole. Add water to cover.

4. Cook in a 350°F oven for about 2 hours, checking occasionally, to make certain it simmers rather than boils. After 2 hours you may proceed to Step 5. Or you may stop the cooking if you plan to serve the dish several hours, or even a day, later.

5. To complete the cooking, add the small onions, mushrooms and chickpeas. Cook for an additional 30 minutes. Keep warm and serve hot.

PARADISE PONTCHEKES
(Photograph on page 30)

Pontchekes are small puffed cakes fried in oil. They resemble doughnuts in texture and look like little balls. Generally, they are made of yeast dough but our recipe calls for no yeast or baking powder. They rise by themselves and taste heavenly. This is why they are called Paradise *Pontchekes.*

For About 40 Pontchekes

1 cup water
4 oz. margarine (1 stick)
1 cup flour
4 eggs
Oil for deep frying

1. Bring the water to a boil. Add margarine and continue boiling until it melts. Add the flour and mix with a wooden spoon until the mixture forms a ball and leaves the sides of the pan.

2. Remove from heat. Beat in the eggs one at a time. Each egg should be completely incorporated before another is added.

3. Heat oil for deep frying. When the oil is hot, drop in dough from a teaspoon or press through a pastry bag. Let puff and turn as needed to assure even browning.

4. Remove from oil with slotted spoon. Drain on paper towels. Serve hot with warm sauce.

DESSERT SAUCES
(Photograph on page 30)

Two sauces for the Paradise *Pontchekes*. Let the guests choose their favorite sauce: chocolate or orange. Accompany with long forks and encourage everybody to dip, fondue style.

Chocolate Sauce
1 cup light corn syrup
2 oz. unsweetened chocolate
1 tsp. vanilla extract
1 tbls. margarine

1. Combine the syrup and chocolate in a sauce pan. Heat over low heat until the chocolate melts.

2. Remove from heat; add the vanilla and margarine. Mix well. Keep warm and serve warm.

Orange Sauce
1 cup orange juice
½ cup sugar
1 tbls. cornstarch
Juice from one lemon
2 tbls. orange liqueur
2 tsp. grated orange rind
1 tbls. margarine

1. Mix the orange juice, sugar and cornstarch in a saucepan. Bring to a boil and boil for 1 minute. Stir constantly to prevent lumps.

2. Remove from heat and let cool a little.

3. Add the margarine, orange liqueur, lemon juice, and orange rind. Mix well.

4. Keep warm and serve warm.

'Say Cheese' Cocktail Party
(Photograph on page 34)

A small cocktail party can be fun for you as well as your guests, if you make things easy on yourself. Let the man in your life handle the bar while you take care of snacks and canapés. Set everything out before your guests arrive then all you have to do is be the hostess with the big, relaxed smile.

Cheese can, indeed, help you smile with its limitless variety of flavors, scents and uses. You can enjoy it 'as is' or use it in cooking and baking. Our menu takes full advantage of cheese's many good qualities with crisp, delicate Tangy Cheese Sticks, piquant Cheese Balls and cubed Cheese and Pickles on Skewers.

To accompany these delicacies we have beautifully decorated canapés featuring: sardines, anchovies and lox. We complete the menu with mustard-brightened Stuffed Eggs, two kinds of olives, small pearl onions, peanuts and a simple dip. For guests who want more cheese we put two big chunks on a tile so they can help themselves.

Arrange snacks on trays that can be passed around or set on a table to which the guests should have free passage. Decorate the serving table with flowers and flickering candles for added charm. (Use the photograph as your guide to decorating and arrangement.)

The drinks in this party are cocktails, of course. But, you don't have to wait for a cocktail party to prepare the cheese and fish snacks. They are delicious any time of the year—on any occasion.

MENU
(planned for 20)

Cheese and Pickles on Skewers*
Cheese Balls*
Stuffed Eggs*
Tangy Cheese Sticks*
Lox Canapés*
Anchovy Canapés*
Sardine Canapés*
Assorted Nuts, Cheeses and Pickles
Simple Dip, Crackers and Potato Chips

Recipe given

CHEESE AND PICKLES ON SKEWERS
(Photograph on page 34)

These cheese-and-pickle snacks serve two purposes: they are a decorative centerpiece and good tasting. Your guests will enjoy nibbling them, especially those who prefer breadless finger foods.

For 1 Skewer

1-2 Swiss cheese cubes
1 olive
1 piece pimiento
1 pearl onion
1 slice pickle
Toothpick or a small decorative skewer

1. Alternate pieces of cheese and pickles on the decorative skewer or toothpick. Try to balance shapes and colors so the result will have 'eye appeal'.

2. Insert the skewers in a big chunk of cheese or in a large grapefruit, and put on a nice plate. Be sure to balance skewers in cheese or grapefruit.

CHEESE BALLS
(Photograph on page 34)

Piquant cheese makes these little balls tangy and appetizing. They can be prepared ahead, and their taste improves with aging.

For 36-40 Balls

4 oz. sharp piquant cheese, grated
2 tbls. butter
½ small onion
Dash pepper
6 oz. cream cheese
1 tbls. brandy
½ cup bread crumbs
2 tbls. finely snipped parsley
Tiny paper cups
Decorated toothpicks

1. Work piquant cheese into the butter in a medium bowl, with a wooden spoon, until smooth. Add the cream cheese and blend thoroughly.

2. Mince onion and add to the cheese-butter mixture with brandy and pepper. Chill for 30 minutes in the refrigerator. The ingredients will harden and you will be able to proceed.

3. Mix the bread crumbs and the snipped parsley on a flat plate. Take the cheese mixture out of the refrigerator. With a teaspoon measure enough cheese for 1 ball and shape between your palms. Roll the ball in the bread crumb mixture to coat completely. Repeat until the cheese is used.

4. Put each ball in a tiny paper cup and insert a decorative toothpick in the center. Arrange on a serving plate. Cover the plate loosely and chill

"SAY CHEESE" COCKTAIL PARTY. A party table laden with appetizing, inviting snacks. From left to right, bottom to top: LOX CANAPÉS (recipe on page 36), cucumber slices topped with carrot rounds and round ANCHOVY CANAPÉS (recipe on page 36). Second row: chunks of cheese hold CHEESE AND PICKLES ON SKEWERS (recipe on page 33) and SARDINE CANAPÉS (recipe on page 36). Third row: green olives, CHEESE BALLS (recipe on page 33) and a simple dip. Fourth row: black olives, STUFFED EGGS (recipe on page 35) and pearl onions. Last row: TANGY CHEESE STICKS (recipe on page 35).

for at least 2 hours. The longer you chill the better, since the flavors have a chance to blend. You may prepare the balls even two days ahead. Serve cold.

STUFFED EGGS
(Photograph on page 34)

An elegant solution to any entertaining problem, eggs can be stuffed and garnished with a variety of fillings. Here we season the stuffing with mustard and garnish half with pimiento strips, and the rest with paprika.

For 24 Pieces

12 large hard-boiled eggs
Mustard filling:
¾ cup mayonnaise
½ cup mustard
¼ tsp. pepper

1. Cook eggs for about 20 minutes. Plunge immediately in cold water for easier peeling.

2. Peel the eggs carefully and cut in halves, lengthwise or crosswise. Take out the yolks without breaking whites.

3. Mash the yolks with a fork or force them through a sieve. Add the other ingredients and mix until smooth.

4. Put the filling in a cake decorating bag with a big star tip and press into the holes of the hard boiled whites. (Or use a teaspoon.)

5. Garnish 12 halves with thin strips of pimento, sprinkle sweet paprika on the rest.

TANGY CHEESE STICKS
(Photograph on page 34)

Two different cheeses are used to make these piquant crisp sticks: cream cheese for flakiness, and sharp Cheddar for color and bright flavor. Wonderful for a party they look particularly pretty when a cluster of them is encircled with a tangy cheese ring.

For 80 Sticks and 8 Rings

2 cups flour
4 oz. butter (½ cup)
3 oz. cream cheese
6 oz. sharp Cheddar cheese
½ tsp. salt
6 tbls. cold water

1. Grate the Cheddar cheese finely into a medium bowl.

2. Put the flour in a large bowl. Cut the butter and the cream cheese into small pieces. Add to the flour. Add the salt.

3. Mix cream cheese into flour with a pastry-blender or your fingers. When it resembles small peas, blend in the grated cheese.

4. Sprinkle the cold water over the mixture to dampen. Form a ball and knead lightly. If the ball does not hold, add 1 or 2 more tablespoons water.

5. Divide dough into 2 balls, wrap in waxed paper and refrigerate for 1 hour or more.

6. Preheat the oven to 450°F and set out 2 big cookie sheets.

7. Remove 1 ball of dough from the refrigerator. Roll out on a lightly floured surface in a rectangle about 8″ x 10″.

8. To cut the rings, use 2 cookie cutters, 3″ and 2″. Cut 6 rings and place on ungreased cookie sheet. Collect leftover dough, roll out again, and make 2 more rings.

9. Take the second ball out of the refrigerator and roll out another rectangle. Cut in 2″ x ½″ strips, using a pastry cutter. Put on the cookie sheet, twisting each strip as you place it down. Continue making the strips until you finish all the dough.

10. Bake for 7 to 9 minutes. The sticks are done when they are golden brown. Cool and store in a tightly closed jar.

To serve, put about 6 sticks through each ring.

Party Canapés

Pretty little canapés that are as piquant and tasty as they are lovely to look at. Try them as a first course for a special dinner, too. Each canapé consists of:

a. thinly sliced bread, cut in decorative shapes
b. flavored butter or spread
c. piquant topping
d. colorful garnish

Our menu uses three kinds of canapés and the ingredients given for them allow two of each kind per guest. Since you know your guests, adjust the variety and quantities to suit your own needs.

Two loaves of regular white bread will be sufficient for the number of canapés given in the recipes. This allows for trimming crusts and cuttting in fancy shapes. (In order not to waste the scraps toast them in a slow oven until nicely browned, then grind to renew your supply of bread crumbs.)

You may do most of the preparations ahead of time. Cut and toast bread a day or two before you need it; stored in an air-tight jar it will stay fresh and crisp. Flavored butter may be fixed early in the day and refrigerated in a closed container; toppings and garnishes should be fixed shortly before assembling, then covered and set in a cool place.

Several hours before serving time, set out all of the prepared ingredients and assemble them carefully to create delicious canapés that will look as though they were made professionally.

LOX CANAPÉS
(Photograph on page 34)

These canapés look handsome topped with squares of bright pink lox. They are tasty, too. They are spread with flavored butter, but you may alternate, and spread them with cream cheese; creating instantly a favorite combination.

For 40 Canapés
10 slices white bread
2 oz. butter (¼ cup)
4 yolks of hard-boiled eggs
2 tbls. mustard
6 oz. lox
Parsley leaves

1. Remove crust from the bread. Cut each slice in 4 equal squares. Arrange on a cookie sheet and toast the squares in a 450°F oven for 7 minutes. Allow to cool.

2. Beat the butter until fluffy, add the egg yolks and mustard. Beat together until smooth.

3. Cut the lox in 1″ squares.

4. Spread the bread squares with the flavored butter. Place a piece of lox on each and garnish with a parsley leaf. Arrange attractively on a tray, cover and chill until serving time.

ANCHOVY CANAPÉS
(Photograph on page 34)

In these canapés the round shape of the bread complements the roundness of the egg-slice and the rolled anchovy topper.

For 40 Canapés
11 slices white bread
4 oz. butter (¼ cup)
2 oz. anchovy paste
4 2-oz. cans rolled anchovies
6 hard-boiled eggs, sliced
1 4-oz. can marinated pimientos

1. With a round cookie cutter or small glass (1½″ diameter) cut 40 rounds from the bread. Toast in the preheated 450°F oven, for 7 minutes.

2. Beat the butter with a wooden spoon until it becomes light and fluffy. Add the anchovy paste and beat until smooth.

3. To assemble canapés use completely cooled bread rounds. Spread each one with the anchovy butter. Lay an egg slice on buttered round then top with a rolled anchovy. Garnish with a small piece of pimiento. Arrange on a tray, cover and chill until serving time.

SARDINE CANAPÉS
(Photograph on page 34)

Fingers of toasted bread spread with sardine-flavored butter, topped by a small whole sardine and trimmed with bits of olive.

For 40 Canapés
14 slices white bread
2 oz. butter (¼ cup)
2 4-oz. cans of Brisling sardines
½ tsp. salt

For garnish:
Black olives
Fresh dill or parsley
Mayonnaise
Tiny lemon wedges

1. Trim the crusts from the bread. Divide each slice into 3 rectangles. Put on a cookie sheet and toast in a 450°F oven for 7 minutes.

2. Drain the sardines. Reserve 40 whole ones and mash the rest to a paste. Beat the butter until fluffy, then mix with the mashed sardines and salt. Cover and set aside or refrigerate.

3. One hour before serving spread bread thinly with the sardine butter. Put a small sardine lengthwise, on each canapé, garnish with a small piece of black olive, a dot of mayonnaise and a leaf of parsley or a tiny sprig of fresh dill. You may also include a very small piece of lemon.

Meaty Snacks-Galore Party

(Photograph on page 38)

Hanukkah arrives the end of December when the year's entertaining season is at its peak. Receptions, parties and impromptu "coffees" are part of this sociable eight-day holiday. These meetings, whether over coffee or stronger refreshments, mold friendships and boost morale.

For an enjoyable evening plan an easy party composed of a variety of snacks and *hors d'oeuvres,* "little somethings" that can be handled with the fingers and eaten in a bite or two. You are not expected to serve these foods formally and guests can use their fingers to their hearts' content. Just be sure to supply plenty of napkins. There are hundreds of recipes for party snacks—hot or cold, fancy or simple, "meaty" or "cheesy." The trick is to choose the ones that fit your mood, your guests and the occasion.

Our *Snacks-Galore* party plays a 'meaty' tune. Everything, except the Avocado Dip, uses meat, chicken, bologna or salami. As shown in the photograph, they are colorful and offer a variety of shapes, flavors and textures: round Aspic Canapés, elongated Bologna 'Horns' filled with zesty mayonnaise salad, dainty cream puffs filled with delicious curried chicken, decorative Egg 'Boats' stuffed with piquant salads and small salami rolls stuffed with pickles.

A hot punch bowl, with or without alcoholic ingredients, is the ideal beverage for evenings when winter winds blow.

MENU
(planned for 20)
Avocado Dip*
Aspic Canapés*
Bologna 'Horns'*
Chicken Curry Puffs*
Egg 'Boats'*
Salami Rolls
Crackers
Relishes
Hot punch
*Recipe given

MEATY 'SNACKS-GALORE' PARTY. The tray holds a few samples of meaty snacks that can be served at a winter party. From left to right: ASPIC CANAPÉS (recipe on page 39), BOLOGNA HORNS (recipe on page 39), CHICKEN-CURRY PUFFS (recipe on page 40), EGG BOATS (recipe on page 40) and salami rolls. To the left of the tray is a bowl of AVOCADO DIP garnished with mushrooms (recipe on page 39). We stick our relishes on toothpicks and then on a green apple-half and finish the table with an inviting bowl of hot punch.

AVOCADO DIP
(Photograph on page 38)

A pleasant change from the cheese-based dips, that goes well with crackers, potato chips or vegetables.

For 2 Medium Bowls

2 avocados
4 tbls. mayonnaise
2 tbls. finely chopped onion
¼ tsp. pepper
½ tsp. salt
2 tbls. lemon juice

Peel avocados, and save the seeds. Mash the flesh and mix in all other ingredients. Bury the seeds in the mixture and cover with plastic wrap; refrigerate. It is best to prepare this dip as close to party time as possible to avoid discoloration, though the seeds and wrap help. Do not forget to remove seeds before serving.

ASPIC CANAPÉS
(Photograph on page 38)

Shimmering aspic encasing egg-slices make these little, round canapés look like jewels on the table. Prepare them at your leisure a day or two before the party, and assemble them when needed.

For 40 Canapés

10 slices rye bread
4 tbls. mayonnaise
2 tbls. mustard

Aspic:
5 cups water
3 tsp. beef bouillon powder
3 tsp. chicken bouillon powder
½ tsp. salt
4 tbls. Sherry
2 tsp. soy sauce
5 tbls. unflavored gelatin (5 envelopes)
7 small hard-boiled eggs
15 pimiento-stuffed olives

1. Prepare the aspic a day or two before the party. You will need a 15″ x 10″ x 1″ jelly-roll pan, a sharp cookie cutter, 1½″ in diameter, and an egg slicer.

2. Measure the water in a medium saucepan. Add the two kinds of bouillon powder, salt, Sherry and soy sauce. Bring to a boil and simmer for 5 minutes.

3. Meantime soften the gelatin in ½ cup water. Stir until completely soft. Add gelatin to the hot

liquid and simer for an additional 3 minutes or until gelatin dissolves completely. Remove from heat. Measure 1 cup and set aside; keep at room temperature.

4. Pour 4 cups of the soup into the jelly-roll pan. Cool until it just begins to set and the surface is sticky to the touch. Slice the eggs with the egg slicer and put 1 slice on top of the aspic. If it sinks to the bottom—the aspic is not set enough, and requires longer cooling.

5. When aspic is ready arrange the egg slices on it in straight rows, 5 slices to a row. You can fit 8 rows in the pan easily. Pour the fifth cup of liquid which should be syrupy, over the egg slices. Tilt the pan gently for even distribution.

6. Cut each olive crosswise into 3's. Tuck 1 slice in the center of each egg slice and press it lightly to make it stick to the gelatin. Cover loosely with waxed paper. Refrigerate for at least 6 hours. It will hold perfectly for as long as 2 days.

7. To assemble the canapés: cut, with 1½″ sharp cookie cutter, 4 rounds out of each slice of bread. Mix the mayonnaise and mustard; spread thinly on the bread rounds.

8. Use the same cookie cutter to cut out aspic covered egg rounds. Be sure each slice is in the center. Lift out with a metal spatula. The first and second aspic rounds will need special attention in removal; the rest will present no problem.

9. Place an aspic round on a bread round. Arrange the canapés on a big tray. Refrigerate until serving time. The canapés will hold nicely for 2 to 3 hours at the party, but do not put near a heater.

BOLOGNA 'HORNS'
(Photograph on page 38)

Appetizing 'horns of plenty' filled with colorful mayonnaise salad.

For 20 'Horns'

20 thin slices of bologna, at least 4″ diameter
20 toothpicks
Mayonnaise salad

To make nice 'horns' you must have large, thin slices of bologna. Fold them over in a cone shape and secure the lower part with a toothpick. Cover and set aside while you make salad.

Mayonnaise Salad

2 8-oz. cans carrots and peas
1 8-oz. can corn
3 hard-boiled eggs
¾ cup mayonnaise
2 small pickles
1 tbls. finely chopped onion
5 parsley sprigs, snipped

Combine all ingredients and put 1 tablespoon in each 'horn'.

CHICKEN CURRY PUFFS

(Photograph on page 38)

Deliciously different, these puffs are easily handled and eaten in one or two bites. Preparation can be done in advance and the final assembly is made at the last minute. Fill puffs with a variety of other fillings, piquant or sweet, as you wish.

For 40 Small Cream Puffs

4 oz. margarine (1 stick)
1 cup boiling water
1 cup flour
½ tsp. salt
Dash nutmeg
4 eggs

1. Preheat the oven to 450°F. Oil a cookie sheet.

2. Combine boiling water and margarine in a saucepan. Heat until the margarine melts. Take off heat and add the flour and seasonings. Return to heat and stir vigorously with a wooden spoon until the mixture forms a ball, and leaves the sides of the pan.

3. Remove from heat, and beat in 1 whole egg, with the wooden spoon until thoroughly blended. Add remaining eggs, one by one, stirring well after each addition. The third and fourth eggs will be a little hard to mix, but keep on until you have a smooth, unified dough.

4. Put small mounds of the dough on the cookie sheet. (You can force them through a cake decorating bag, or drop them from a teaspoon.) They should be about 1″ in diameter, spread 2″ apart.

5. Bake in a hot oven for about 20 minutes. They have to puff and turn golden brown. Pierce them with a sharp knife to let the steam escape so the puff will stay crisp.

6. Return to the oven, turn off the heat, and leave the door ajar. Dry out the puffs for another 20 minutes.

7. Keep the puffs crisp in a tightly covered jar.

8. Before serving remove the top, fill the bottom with chicken curry salad (which you can prepare hours ahead) and replace the top.

Chicken Curry Salad

1½ cups diced, cooked chicken
2 tbls. finely chopped onion
½ cup mayonnaise
1 hard-boiled egg, grated
1 tsp. salt
½ tsp. curry powder
Dash pepper

Mix all ingredients, and fill the puffs.

EGG 'BOATS'

(Photograph on page 38)

These stuffed eggs are very colorful, filled as they are with zesty salads, then garnished with olives and pickles. They blend very well with the rest of the party menu, too.

For 20 Pieces

10 eggs
Horseradish filling (below)
Mayonnaise salad (See Index)
10 black olives
1 pickle, sliced

1. Use the freshest eggs possible and cook 20 minutes. Plunge immediately in cold water for easier peeling.

2. Peel the eggs carefully; cut in halves and lift out yolks without breaking whites. Set aside while you make horseradish filling and mayonnaise salad.

Horseradish Filling

10 yolks (of the hard-boiled eggs)
½ cup mayonnaise
3 tbls. horseradish with beets
½ tsp. salt

1. Mash yolks and combine with remaining ingredients. Blend well.

2. Fill 10 egg halves with horseradish filling; garnish with pickle slices.

3. Fill remaining halves with mayonnaise salad; garnish with olives. Cover and chill until serving time.

V

TU BISHEVAT:
GOING ON A 'NATURE KICK'

Tu bishevat salutes nature and is known as the New Year for Trees. It is celebrated for one day only and its name literally means The Fifteenth of the Hebrew months of *Shevat,* which is also its date. This holiday marks the beginning of spring in Israel. After the barren winter nature awakens: trees bud, the sun shines, birds sing; Meadows, orchards and vineyards begin to blossom. Mother Nature starts a new cycle, a new year and *Tu Bishevat* says 'Happy Birthday' to her.

The love and concern for nature, particularly trees, is expressed by planting saplings on *Tu Bishevat.* Adults and youngsters go to parks, fields and young forests to plant them with their own hands. For Jewish people who lived through many generations far away from their country *Tu Bishevat* has always been a reminder that once they had a land of their own and observing the customs was a symbol of hope that they would come back and live on their own soil once again.

Foods of the holiday are related to nature and trees as well. During *Tu Bishevat* it is traditional to serve fruits. Since few are available fresh at this time of year dried varieties are most often used: raisins, dates, carobs, prunes, nuts, dried figs and apricots, to name a few. The *Tu Bishevat* dried fruits are sometimes called *Hamishah Asar* (fifteen, in Hebrew), referring to the date of the holiday.

Homemade Nature Sweets

(Photograph on page 42)

Dried fruits bring a wealth of delicious serving possibilities: use them as is, or turn them into light desserts to end any meal on a sweet note. They can accompany coffee instead of cakes, or, you may arrange them neatly on a plate to be given as a 'nature candy box.' You will find that the homemade, 'natural' candies and sweets are welcomed even by those who generally push away the conventional desserts.

To make a 'nature candy box,' put a paper doily on a straw plate and arrange dried fruits and nuts in it. (Follow the patterns in the picture or create your own designs.) You may wish to add some of the 'Homemade Nature Sweets' as well. Complete

TU BISHEVAT—THE NATURE-KICK HOLIDAY. A table loaded with fruits, nuts, budding branches and dried plants is the background for Homemade Nature Sweets that are featured in the center straw plate (recipes begin on page 43). In the middle of the plate is a small FRUIT CAKE FOR TU BISHEVAT (recipe on page 45), while the silver dish at the rear holds a Charlotte, a non-bake delicious cake, filled with chunks of candied fruits (recipe on page 45). Left Fruit Plate, Clockwise: Figs, Prunes, Almonds, Candied orange rind, Candied cherries, Raisins, Apricots, Candied pears, Dates, Walnuts. Right Fruit Plate, Clockwise: Prunes, Candied cherries, Prunes, Fig rolls, Prunes, Figs and pecans, Prunes, Apricot fruit roll, Apricots (in center).

your gift with a cover of clear plastic topped with a festive bow. Accompany it with a personal greeting card to make it yours alone.

Homemade Nature Sweets come in a variety of fruity flavors. There is little work involved in preparation and absolutely no cooking or baking. Assemble and shape the various ingredients letting the fruits' textures, colors and tastes speak for themselves. Five different sweets are shown in the center plate of the picture. They can be done according to the following recipes.

HOMEMADE NATURE SWEETS
(clockwise, on center plate)

Date Fingers*
Prune-Almond Sweets*
Date-Fig-Walnut Treats*
Fig-Cherry Bonbons*
Apricot 'Blossom' Balls*

*Recipe given

DATE 'FINGERS'
(Photograph on page 42)

When you bite into these nature candies you will experience a triple sensation. Three major ingredients will attract your attention simultaneously: the sweetness of the ground dates, the crunchiness of the blanched almonds and the specific tingle of the ground coconut.

For About 20 Fingers

8 oz. dates, pitted
4 oz. ground coconut
2 tbls. bread crumbs
2 tsp. lemon juice
20 blanched whole almonds (about 1 oz.)
20 small paper cups

1. Grind the dates in a food chopper; if the coconut is not ground fine enough put in half of it at the same time. Next put through 1 tablespoon bread crumbs to push down any fruit left in the machine. Put everything in a medium bowl.

2. Add the lemon juice and the remaining bread crumbs to the bowl. Mix well with a wooden spoon until the mixture forms a smooth 'dough.'

3. Take 1 heaping teaspoon of the 'dough' and shape, between your hands, a 'finger,' about 2" long. To use an assembly-line method: divide 'dough' in quarters and roll each quarter on a bread board to form a rope, thick as your finger and 10" long. Cut at 2" intervals. Repeat with the rest of the 'dough.'

4. Sprinkle the remaining 2 ounces coconut on a flat plate. (If it is not very fine, or if you use coconut flakes, grind quickly in a blender first.)

5. Coat the date 'fingers' with coconut, place each one in a paper cup and tuck in an almond for garnish.

PRUNE-ALMOND SWEETS
(Photograph on page 42)

Combine the smooth tartness of dark, dried prunes and the fragile crunchiness of white almonds to have a winning combination—especially for those who are short of time.

For 20 Sweets
40 medium prunes, pitted (about 1 lb.)
8 oz. good apricot jam
20 whole blanched almonds (about 1 oz.)
20 small paper cups

1. Put a prune in each paper cup. Spread with jam.

2. Top with another prune. Press together with your fingers. Spread the top prune with more jam and tuck an almond on top.

DATE-FIG-WALNUT TREATS
(Photograph on page 42)

These sweets are fingers of luscious, sweet smooth date-fig mixture, dipped in chopped walnuts just to trap some nutty chunks for the enjoyment of the gourmet.

For About 20 Pieces
4 oz. dates, pitted
4 oz. figs
2 tbls. bread crumbs
2 tsp. lemon juice
1 tsp. brandy
4 oz. chopped walnuts
20 small paper cups

1. Remove the stems from the figs. Put figs through a meat grinder with the dates. Add 1 tablespoon bread crumbs to the grinder to push down any leftovers. Put all in a medium bowl.

2. Add the lemon juice and brandy; mix well with a wooden spoon. Add the remaining bread crumbs and blend until a smooth 'dough' forms.

3. Take a heaping teaspoon of the 'dough' and shape between your hands in a 'finger' 1½" long.

Repeat until all 'dough' is used. Assembly-line method: divide dough in thirds and roll each part on a bread board to form a rope ¾" thick. Cut it in 7 even pieces.

4. Spread the chopped walnuts on a flat plate. Press each 'finger' on the nuts to cover one side only. Place walnut-side up, on a paper cup.

FIG-CHERRY BONBONS
(Photograph on page 42)

These are deliciously sticky bonbons in which dried figs and candied cherries are 'married' by the good orange marmalade. Quick to prepare, they fit perfectly with a carefree holiday mood.

For 20 Bonbons
40 medium figs (about 1½ lb.)
10 oz. good orange marmalade
20 candied cherries (about 4 oz.)
20 small paper cups

1. Put 1 fig in each paper cup. Top with some marmalade.

2. Make a small incision in the remaining figs. Put ½ teaspoon marmalade in each of them. Tuck a cherry on top.

3. Put the filled figs on top of those in the paper cups. Press with your fingers to 'glue' the two together.

APRICOT 'BLOSSOM' BALLS
(Photograph on page 42)

The tartness, special color, flavor and texture of the ground dried apricots is complemented by the white flaky coconut to make an excellent natural candy.

For About 20 Balls
8 oz. apricots, dried
6 oz. coconut flakes
1 tbls. orange marmalade
2 tbls. bread crumbs
1 tsp. orange liqueur
20 tiny paper cups

1. Put the apricots and half of the coconut through a meat grinder. Follow with 1 tablespoon bread crumbs to push down the leftovers. Put everything in a medium bowl.

2. Add the marmalade, orange liqueur and remaining bread crumbs. Mix well with a wooden spoon until a smooth 'dough' forms.

3. Put half of the 'dough' on a piece of waxed paper, fold the paper over it and shape into a rope of 10″. (The waxed paper will prevent the 'dough' from sticking to your hands.) Remove the paper and cut the 'rope' in 10 pieces. Shape each piece in a ball. Repeat with the rest.

4. Spread the remaining coconut flakes on a flat plate. Roll the 'blossom' balls in the flakes and put in paper cups.

Tu Bishevat Cakes

NON-BAKE DELICIOUS CAKE
(Photograph on page 42)

This dessert cake is known as "Charlotte" or "Diplomat" and is outstanding with either name. It is made in a mold lined with ladyfingers and filled with a mousse-like concoction that actually melts in your mouth. Candied fruits are nestled there, adding flavor, texture and color. We have tried this classic non-bake cake with the non-dairy type whipped cream and enjoyed good results which means you can even end a 'meaty' dinner with it.

½ cup dried, candied fruits
¼ cup orange liqueur
1½ tbls. unflavored gelatin
1/3 cup cold water
5 egg yolks
1/3 cup sugar
1 tbls. flour
1 cup milk (or non-dairy milk)
48 ladyfingers
2 cups whipping cream (or non-dairy whipping cream)

For garnish:
12 candied cherries
4 mint leaves

1. Cut the candied fruit into very small pieces and soak in orange liqueur. (You can use dates, figs, raisins, cherries, and orange rind.)

2. Put the gelatin in the water to soften.

3. Whip the egg yolks with the sugar until lemon-colored and thick. Beat in the flour.

4. Bring the milk to a boil and add, in a slow stream to the egg yolks. Beat constantly. Stir in the softened gelatin. Put the mixture on a very low heat, or better yet, on top of a double boiler. Bring to a gentle boil while stirring constantly. (Heavy boiling will curdle the eggs.) It is ready when the gelatin dissolves completely and the mixture thickens enough to coat a metal spoon.

5. Remove from heat and strain through a fine sieve into a clean bowl. Cool.

6. While the yolk mixture cools line the bottom of an 8″ springform pan with a round piece of waxed paper. With sharp knife cut the ladyfingers diagonally to resemble long triangles and arrange them on the bottom of the mold. Put the wide side toward the 'walls' of the mold and the points toward the center. Stand whole ladyfingers upright around 'walls' of mold.

7. Whip the cream until it holds its shape.

8. Add the fruits, and the liqueur in which they were soaked, to completely cooled egg mixture. Reserve one-fourth of the whipped cream for garnish; fold remainder into egg mixture gently. Fold only until there is no trace of cream.

9. Pour half the mixture into the lined pan. Cover with a layer of ladyfingers which does not have to be in perfect order, and add the remaining filling. Arrange the rest of the ladyfingers on top. Cover with waxed paper and chill overnight.

10. To unmold, run a knife around the sides of mold to loosen the cake. Invert on a serving plate, release the springform, lift off bottom and remove the waxed paper. The top of the cake is the nicely arranged ladyfinger bottom.

11. To garnish, cut the 12 candied cherries into halves. Use a pastry bag to press 'roses' from the reserved whipped cream around the cake rim; make a big one in the center. Top with the cherries and mint leaves. Chill until serving time.

FRUIT CAKE FOR TU BISHEVAT
(Photograph on page 42)

This fruit cake is based on some of the traditional fruits for *Tu Bishevat,* but you can add other fruits, too. In our picture is appears in the center of the 'Homemade Sweets Plate' in a small paper cup; it can be baked in a loaf pan as well. This cake keeps very well, and even improves by aging.

For a 9″ x 5″ x 3″ Loaf or 15 Individual Cakes

¾ cup brown sugar, firmly packed
1 egg
3 tbls. margarine
1 cup warm water
2½ cups flour
2 tsp. baking powder
1½ tsp. baking soda
1 cup chopped dried fruit (dates, figs)
½ cup chopped walnuts

1. Mix the brown sugar, egg and margarine together in a large bowl. Add the warm water and continue mixing until unified.

2. Measure the flour, baking powder and baking soda. Sift together into the bowl. Mix well.

3. Cut or chop the dried fruit in small pieces, pack firmly in the measuring cup.

4. Add the fruit and nuts to the batter. Mix well.

5. Grease loaf pan very generously and fill with the batter. Let stand for 15 minutes then decorate with 8 slices of dates. For individual cakes, place small paper cups in a muffin tin, fill with the batter and decorate with date slivers.

6. Bake in a 350°F oven for 40 to 80 minutes (depending on the size), or until a wooden toothpick comes out dry. Remove from pan and cool.

VI

PURIM: GOODIES FOR THE KIDDIES

PURIM IS THE JOLLIEST, most light-hearted and child-oriented holiday on the Jewish calendar. It is a good day for the youngsters because they are allowed, in fact even encouraged, to don masks and costumes: they can be kings, queens, dragons, astronauts, pirates, ballerinas—whatever strikes their fancy. This is the day when the efforts of mother and child in planning and making an interesting costume get a public showing.

Although *Purim* comes at a time when spring showers and sunny days have equal chances, the youngsters pay no attention to the weather. They get into their costumes and parade through city streets to see—and be seen—by all.

As with most Jewish holidays *Purim* has ancient roots. It is a happy celebration commemorating events that occurred some twenty-four centuries ago when the Jews lived in Persia. The Persian king, Ahasuerus, had been convinced by his sneaky advisor Haman to eliminate all of the Jews in his realm. Esther, a beautiful young Jewish girl who had been chosen as the king's wife, learned of the plot from her wise uncle Mordecai and petitioned the king in behalf of her people. She succeeded in persuading Ahasuerus to reverse his decision, thus saving the Jews from total disaster. This happy end came on *Purim,* the day the Jews were scheduled for extinction; which is why the holiday is celebrated with such gaiety.

The entire story of *Purim* is told in the Book of Esther and it is customary to read the book on the eve of the holiday to the accompaniment of a jolly tune written especially for the occasion. It should be noted that this book of the Bible is inscribed on a long narrow scroll, called a *Megilah* in Hebrew, that is encased in an ornamented container. (A *Megilah* appears in the photograph near the chick and a special *Purim* toy, the *Ra'ashan,* or noisemaker, is in front of the train.) During the reading of the *Megilah* children shake the *Ra'ashan* vigorously every time the name of Haman is mentioned.

The celebration of *Purim* is unique among Jewish holidays: drinking, playing, joking and eating are the order of the day and the wearing of costumes makes it even easier to forget formality. *Mishloach Manot* (sending of gifts in Hebrew), is a tradition, too. Cakes and sweets are exchanged among friends, and gifts of money are made to the poor, with the costumed children acting as delivery messengers.

Hamantashen is the most famous traditional food of *Purim* and we begin this chapter with a recipe for these small triangular cakes, as well as an explanation of their name. The remaining pages are devoted to fun in the kitchen with fanciful cakes, cookies, sweets and treats for the entire family.

Purim Specialty

HAMANTASHEN
(Photograph on page 56)

Hamantashen are small triangular cakes that resemble tricorn hats. The name means Haman's Pockets, after Haman, the advisor to the king of ancient Persia. In Hebrew they are called *Oznei Haman*, meaning Haman's Ears. The little delicious dough pockets are filled with a rich, black, moist poppy seed concoction. You can see two of them in the picture, serving as shoes for the Popped Corn King.

The yeast dough used in making the *Hamantashen* is a basic one, suitable for many applications including The Frightful Crocodile and the Friendly Turtle, described later on.

For About 3 Dozen

Basic Yeast Dough
½ cup warm water
½ cup lukewarm milk
1 cake fresh yeast (0.6 oz.)
½ cup sugar
½ tsp. salt
2 eggs at room temperature
2 oz. soft butter (¼ cup)
4½-5 cups regular flour
1 tsp. vanilla
1 tsp. grated lemon rind
2 drops yellow food coloring

1. Dissolve the yeast in the warm water. Combine in a large mixing bowl with the milk, sugar, salt and about half of the flour. Mix and let rest for 10 minutes in a warm place.

2. Add the eggs, vanilla, food coloring, soft butter and grated lemon rind. Stir in enough of the remaining flour to make the dough manageable. Knead about 8 minutes until the dough is smooth and elastic. Shape into a ball.

3. Put a few drops of oil in a clean bowl and grease completely. Place the dough in it, turning once to grease the top. Let stand in a warm place about 1½ hours until the ball doubles.

4. Punch down then knead lightly for 3 minutes. Let rise again for 45 minutes then punch down and shape into a ball. The dough is now ready for use.

To Assemble the Hamantashen

1. Preheat the oven to 325°F. Prepare the Poppy Seed Filling (recipe follows). Lightly oil 2 cookie sheets.

2. Roll the dough to ⅛″ thickness. Cut out rounds 4″ in diameter, using a coffee cup as your cookie cutter. Put a teaspoonful of the filling in the center of each round. Moisten the edges with a beaten egg then lift them from 3 points and pinch together to form a triangle. Pinch the edges again to seal tightly and prevent the filling from leaking out.

3. Put the *Hamantashen* on the cookie sheets and brush their tops with milk or egg beaten with water. Bake for about 25 minutes or until golden brown.

Poppy Seed Filling
1 cup milk
8 oz. poppy seed (1½ cups)
1 tbls. butter
3 tbls. raisins
4 tbls. honey
4 tbls. sugar
2 tsp. lemon juice
1 tsp. grated lemon rind

1. Boil the milk with the sugar, poppy seed and butter. Reduce the heat and cook gently until all the milk is absorbed. Add the remaining ingredients and mix well. Cool thoroughly before using.

Cakes in Disguise
(Photograph on page 52)

In the merry spirit of *Purim,* which is as jolly as a happy carnival, we borrow a note from the children and put regular year-round cakes in costume, too.

These unusually shaped cakes help you make *Purim's* good mood even better; the smiles, compliments and thanks they will bring are well worth the effort of making them. Best of all, preparation is really much easier than one might think. Once you do them for *Purim* you will find many other good reasons for making them throughout the year. Little boys—their fathers, too—will be delighted with a chocolate covered Choo-Choo Train as a birthday cake. Girls will adore the Pink Butterfly, as will grandmother on Mother's Day, and everyone will be partial to the Furry Bunny or Yellow Chick who can turn an ordinary occasion into a super celebration.

Cakes in disguise are exactly what their name suggests: regular cakes, cleverly cut and decorated to give them new personalities. No special pans or tools are needed. Patterns and detailed instructions are given here. Try them and see how they fill your *Purim* with joy and laughter.

Cake Sculpturing

Making the disguised cakes will give you a good feeling of being creative and artistic. You will do some cutting and shaping, some coloring and decorating, and by just using your hands you will create imaginative unusual forms out of ordinary cakes.

The basic materials for cake sculpturing are simple. Sponge cake, baked in either a round or a square pan is your primary construction material. You could bake your own, using the Basic Sponge Cake recipe given here or, start with store-bought sponge cake or packaged mix. For easier cutting and shaping let the cakes be one day old and a little dry. The other materials used are frostings, icings and decorations that combined make your creations look even more life-like.

HOW TO USE PATTERNS: Copy the pattern for the cake selected on waxed or tracing paper; cut pattern in separate pieces along solid lines with scissors.

HOW TO CUT CAKES: Arrange pattern pieces on top of cake, using drawings as your guide. Hold knife perpendicular and cut around pattern. Treat young ones to the leftovers that are marked "X" on the pattern. (They are certain to be on hand to watch the miracles you are about to perform.)

HOW TO ASSEMBLE CAKES: Prepare a flat serving tray or plate. If you don't have one big enough, make it of cardboard and cover with colorful construction paper, waxed paper or aluminum foil.

Assemble cut pieces of cake on serving plate as indicated in drawing. Make sure all parts stand up straight and are symmetrical. If not use your knife to flatten the base and correct shapes. (Minor defects can be overcome with a coating of frosting.) Place strips of waxed paper under edges of cake to catch spilled frosting so that the platter will stay clean; remove after cake is decorated.

Cover body or base of cakes with a layer of frosting. Attach feet, wings, wedges, etc., as specified in diagram. (A toothpick here and there may be helpful in holding things together.) Give additions an initial layer of frosting.

Once assembled, cover entire cake with a second layer of frosting. Add decorations, consulting the picture for proper location. You don't have to copy exactly. Improvise. Let your creative talent and the *Purim* spirit guide you to innovations of your own.

CAKES IN DISGUISE
(instructions given)

The Pink Butterfly
The Furry Bunny
The Yellow Chick
The Choo Choo Train

THE PINK BUTTERFLY
(Photograph on page 52)

The butterfly is the simplest of the sculptured cakes. The clever cutting of the round cake makes use of every crumb without any leftovers. It has an unusual pink frosting that contains no butter or margarine, yet keeps its shape and bubbly structure.

1 9″ Round Cake

Pink frosting:

1 3-oz. pkg. strawberry or cherry gelatin
1 cup whipping cream

Decorating materials:

2 pipe cleaners, for the antennae
6 elongated chocolate-covered orange rind,
    for bordering the body
Assorted colorful candies, for designs on the wings

1. Prepare a 9″ round cake. It can be store-bought, made out of a mix, or baked according to Basic Sponge Cake recipe given in this chapter.

2. Prepare the frosting: make the gelatin according to package directions. Cool until sticky, but not firm. Whip the cream until it holds its shape. Whip the partially set gelatin and fold into the whipped cream. Cool while you cut and assemble the butterfly.

3. Cut the cake following the general instructions for cake sculpturing.

4. Spread the pink frosting over the top and sides of the butterfly before the frosting gets set.

5. Follow the photograph to insert the pipe cleaners in the head, and for placement of the other decorating materials on the body and wings of the butterfly. The simple round cake can now 'fly' to a *Purim* ball.

2. Prepare the white frosting; beat the margarine until fluffy. Sift the sugar and add, alternately with the milk, to margarine, beating after each addition. Add the vanilla extract and continue beating for 3 minutes.

3. Cut the cake, following the general instructions for cake sculpturing.

4. Remove 3 tablespoons white frosting to a small plate and add 1 drop of red food coloring. Mix well. Use for the bunny's ears.

5. Frost the bunny twice, as directed, with the remaining white frosting. Cover the designated areas of the bunny's ears with the pink frosting.

6. Cover the entire body with the coconut flakes to represent fur. Press the coconut flakes slightly into the white frosting with your fingers, and attach the eyes and nose.

THE FURRY BUNNY
(Photograph on page 52)

The bunny has pink frosted ears, fur of coconut flakes and a mouth of chocolate candy. Sweet and cute, he will amuse children of all ages on *Purim* or on their own birthdays.

1 9″ Round Cake

White frosting:
4 oz. unsalted margarine (1 stick)
1 lb. confectioners' sugar (4½ cups)
3 tbls. milk
1½ tsp. vanilla extract
6 oz. flaked coconut (2 cups)

Decorating materials:
2 red gum drops, for the eyes
1 chocolate candy, for the mouth
1 drop red food coloring

1. Prepare a 9″ round cake. It can be store bought, made out of a mix, or baked according to Basic Sponge Cake recipe, given in this chapter.

CAKES IN DISGUISE. Four costumed cakes surround an ancient Megilah, which contains the story of Purim. They are: THE PINK BUTTERFLY (recipe on page 50), THE YELLOW CHICK (recipe on page 54), THE CHOO CHOO TRAIN (recipe on page 54) and THE FURRY BUNNY (recipe on page 51). On the left are three SMILING CHOCOLATE CLOWNS (recipe on page 59). On the right front corner is a Ra'ashan, noisemaker used by children through this happy holiday.

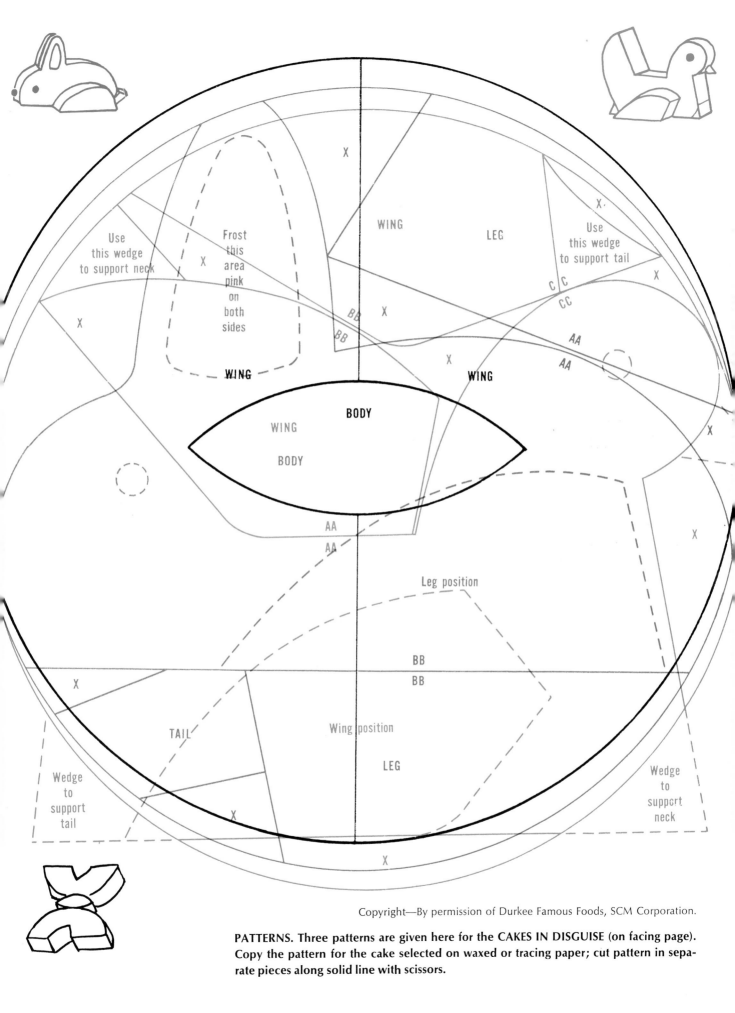

X

WING   LEG

Use
this wedge
to support neck

Frost
this
area
pink
on
both
sides

X   Use
this wedge
to support tail

X

X

X   X

X

BB
BB   X   CC
CC
CC

AA
AA

WING   WING

X

BODY

WING

BODY   X

AA
AA

X

Leg position

BB
BB

X

TAIL   Wing position

LEG

Wedge
to
support
tail

Wedge
to
support
neck

X

X

PATTERNS. Three patterns are given here for the CAKES IN DISGUISE (on facing page). Copy the pattern for the cake selected on waxed or tracing paper; cut pattern in separate pieces along solid line with scissors.

THE YELLOW CHICK
(Photograph on page 52)

Let this sculptured chick roost over your *Purim* party or be the centerpiece for a family celebration. Give it plenty of chocolate candy 'grains,' and keep an eye on the almond-candy 'eggs.'

1 9" Round Cake

Yellow frosting:
4 oz. unsalted margarine (1 stick)
3 yolks
1 lb. confectioners' sugar (4½ cups)
1 tsp. vanilla extract
2 drops yellow food coloring

Decorating materials:
1 red marmalade candy, for the comb
1 cone-shaped red gum drop, for the beak
2 candies, for eyes

1. Prepare a 9" round cake. It can be store bought, made out of a mix, or baked according to Basic Sponge Cake recipe in this chapter.

2. Prepare the yellow frosting: Beat the margarine until fluffy. Add the egg yolks one at a time, beating after each addition. Beat in the sugar, vanilla extract, and food coloring. Beat for 3 more minutes.

3. Cut the cake, following the general instructions for cake sculpturing.

4. Frost the chick twice, as directed, then give it a 'feathery' look using a fork, to make grooves in the body, tail and wings.

5. Cut the red marmalade candy in shape of the chick's comb; attach it to the head.

6. Insert a toothpick in the gum drop and stick in chick's head as the beak. Attach the eyes by pressing them into the frosting.

7. Spread some almond-candy 'eggs' near the chick, and some colorful candy 'food' before it.

THE CHOO CHOO TRAIN
(Photograph on page 52)

The little train is ideal for *Purim*, as well as for little boys' parties. The cutting and assembling is quite easy, and the key to this cake's success is using the most realistic looking trimmings and decorations.

1 Recipe Basic Sponge Cake

Chocolate icing:
12 oz. semi-sweet chocolate
7 tbls. water
2 oz. unsalted margarine (½ stick)
¼ cup confectioners' sugar

Red frosting:
2 oz. unsalted margarine (½ stick)
1 cup confectioners' sugar
3 drops vanilla extract
2 drops red food coloring

Decorating materials:
22 round 1" pretzels, for the wheels
12 flat sugar wafers, for windows
2 white chocolate candies, for the headlights
1 red pipe cleaner, for the smoke
1 chocolate coated wafer, for the chimney
Elongated chocolate candies, or licorice, for the tracks

1. Make the sponge cake as directed and bake in a greased 13" x 9" x 2" pan. Cool completely before using.

2. Prepare the chocolate icing: melt the chocolate with water in top of a double boiler. Remove from heat and add the sugar alternately with pieces of the margarine. Mix well after each addition. Keep over hot, not boiling, water, while you cut the cake.

3. Cut the cake lengthwise into 3 3" strips. Cut 2 strips in half, to make 4 cars. The third strip is for the locomotive. Use the photograph as your guide for shaping it.

4. Put the 4 cars on waxed paper and coat them with the chocolate icing. For even icing, repeat the coating operation again.

5. Prepare the red frosting: beat all frosting ingredients thoroughly. Frost front part of the locomotive with red frosting, and coat the rest twice, with chocolate icing.

6. Attach the wheels and windows before the icing hardens.

7. With the locomotive leading the way assemble the cars on a big tray or a piece of covered cardboard. Add the chocolate wafers as the chimney, white chocolate candies as the headlights, and twisted red pipe cleaner as the unpolluting smoke.

Cooky Masquerade Ball

(Photograph on page 56)

Cakes, cookies and other goodies join the jolly mood of *Purim* with a merry masquerade of their own: Frightful Crocodiles dance with Jumping Frogs, Busy Bees buzz around a plump Popped Corn King, Little Flat Clowns form a barber-shop quartet, while Cream-Filled Swans float serenely before the crowd. Only the Wise Owls look worried, but they will cheer up after a glass or two.

As at a real costume party we conducted a 'contest' when testing our recipes to choose winners on the basis of beauty, originality, ease of preparation and versatility of materials. Among the ten selected, you will find only four need baking. The rest are fashioned from ready-made candies, cookies and other edible goodies such as nuts.

The Crocodile and Tortoise are made of yeast dough, the Little Clowns of sugar dough and the gracious Swans of cream puff dough. Our Owls and Frogs are glued together from store-bought cookies and candies while other candies and nuts produce the Small Turtles and the Busy Bees. Mock Marzipan Fruits and a Popped Corn King complete our winning list.

Nor will you be alone in the kitchen when you make frolicsome 'costume cookies' for *Purim*. Every member of the family will be right there to get in on his share of the fun—building, drawing, pasting, decorating, coloring, cutting and shaping these exciting treats. Before you can say 'Happy *Purim*' everyone will be so absorbed in this creative cookery you could quietly sneak out to a matinée.

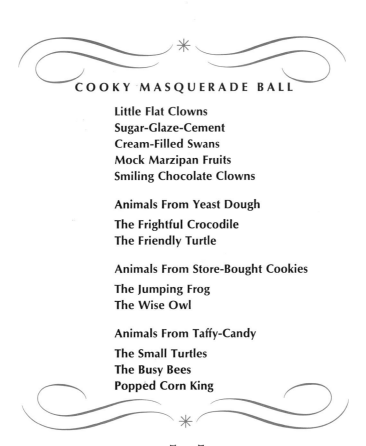

COOKY MASQUERADE BALL

Little Flat Clowns
Sugar-Glaze-Cement
Cream-Filled Swans
Mock Marzipan Fruits
Smiling Chocolate Clowns

Animals From Yeast Dough

The Frightful Crocodile
The Friendly Turtle

Animals From Store-Bought Cookies

The Jumping Frog
The Wise Owl

Animals From Taffy-Candy

The Small Turtles
The Busy Bees
Popped Corn King

A COOKY MASQUERADE BALL. Here is a parade of all the costumed cookies. In the back row, from left to right are two WISE OWLS (recipe on page 62), The LITTLE FLAT CLOWNS (recipe on page 57), the POPPED CORN KING (recipe on page 63) and a formation of BUSY BEES (recipe on page 62). In the front row are the MOCK MARZIPAN FRUITS (recipe on page 59) and the FRIENDLY TURTLE (recipe on page 61) who is watching a group of taffy SMALL TURTLES (recipe on page 62). In the center of the picture are the CREAM-FILLED SWAN floating proudly (recipe on page 58), the JUMPING FROGS (recipe on page 61), and the FRIGHTFUL CROCODILE (recipe on page 60).

LITTLE FLAT CLOWNS
(Photograph on page 56)

The little clowns will delight everyone. They are made of sugar dough, and decorated with colorful glaze. Part of the dough can be given to the children to roll it out and shape to their hearts' content.

For Over 30 Cookies

2 cups flour
1 cup sugar
4 oz. margarine (1 stick)
1 tsp. baking powder
1 egg
1 tsp. vanilla extract
Dash salt
Sugar-Glaze-Cement (see next)

1. Lightly grease 2 large cookie sheets. Preheat oven to 400°F. Take the margarine out of the refrigerator, and let soften to room temperature.

2. Mix the flour and salt in a large bowl. Add the sugar and pieces of the softened margarine. Mix vigorously with a wooden spoon. Add the egg, vanilla and baking powder and continue mixing until the mixture crumbles and resembles little peas.

3. Knead with your hands, pressing the crumbs together for a few minutes until a smooth, elastic dough forms. If it gets too soft for handling cool in the refrigerator for 15 minutes or until the margarine hardens.

4. Divide the dough into 3 equal parts, shape into balls and wrap. Keep 2 balls in the refrigerator while working on the third. Roll each ball out on a floured surface to an even 1/8" thickness. Cut out the clowns according to pattern given, or cut with a man-shaped cookie cutter.

5. Arrange the clowns on the cookie sheet. Bake for about 7 minutes. The clowns should be very pale brown. Repeat the rolling and cutting until all dough is used. While one cookie sheet is in the oven arrange the cookies on the other sheet. This saves time and lets you put one sheet in the oven as soon as you remove the other.

6. Cool the baked cookies on a wire rack. When completely cool and crisp, decorate with the colorful Sugar-Glaze-Cement, using the picture as your guide.

To Make A Clown Pattern

Trace the pattern given on transparent paper. Paste on a piece of cardboard and cut out. It is wise to paste and fold a piece of aluminum foil around the edges of the pattern to avoid greasy stains.

To Cut The Clowns

Put the pattern on the dough and cut around it with a sharp, pointed knife. Hold knife as straight up as possible.

SUGAR-GLAZE-CEMENT

This little recipe is great in the kitchen. Use it for decorating cakes and cookies. By adding a few drops of food coloring it will turn to any desired shade and make decorating great fun. The glaze is also wonderful for holding things together, when making Jumping Frogs or Wise Owls out of store-bought cookies. It will actually 'cement' the ingredients to one another.

1 cup confectioners' sugar
1 egg white
½ tsp. cream of tartar

1. Put the egg white in a bowl. Add the sugar; mix, then begin to whip. Add the cream of tartar and continue whipping until very thick, but still spreadable.

2. Transfer immediately to a jar that can be tightly sealed. Take out only the amount needed and store remainder in the closed jar.

3. To use for glazing transfer a small amount to a little plate. Add the color you need, mix and use immediately. If it hardens add a few drops of water and re-mix. Push through pastry bags fitted with very small tips, to trim and decorate.

4. To use as a cement: spread some glaze where it is needed and attach to other ingredient immediately. Let stand undisturbed until set.

CREAM-FILLED SWANS
(Photograph on page 56)

A classic, continental dessert that can be prepared easily at home. Just follow the instructions and drawing to have stately cream-filled swans reigning over your tray of sweets. Fill your swans with whipped cream, ice cream or pudding; dust them with confectioners' sugar, or cover with chocolate sauce. Any way you choose will bring you praises.

For 8 Swans

4 oz. margarine (1 stick)
1 cup boiling water
1 cup flour
½ tsp. salt
⅛ tsp. nutmeg
4 eggs

The filling:

1 cup whipping cream
2 tbls. confectioners' sugar
1 tsp. vanilla extract

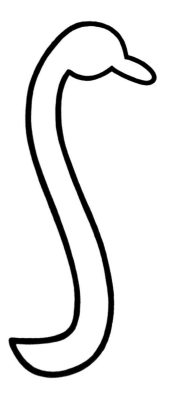

1. Combine the boiling water and margarine in a saucepan and heat until the margarine melts. Remove from heat; add the flour and seasonings. Return to heat and stir vigorously with a wooden spoon until a ball forms.

2. Remove from heat. Add 1 whole egg and stir with the wooden spoon until thoroughly incorporated. Add the remaining 3 eggs one at a time, stirring well after each addition. The third and fourth eggs will be a little harder to mix. Keep on until you have a smooth, unified dough.

3. Copy the shape of swan neck and head on transparent paper. Glue to a piece of cardboard, and cut out. Now you have a pattern you can use again and again.

4. Preheat the oven to 400°F.

5. Place a piece of aluminum foil on a cookie sheet. Put the pattern on the foil and trace around it with a ballpoint pen. (A pencil tends to tear the foil.) Draw 8 necks.

6. Put part of dough in a pastry bag. Follow the shape of the neck with the tip of the bag, pressing out just enough dough to fill the drawing. Add an extra drop of dough to the top of the head to make it a little thicker.

[58]

7. Bake the necks for about 20 minutes, until golden brown.

8. Divide the remaining dough in 8 parts. Drop them on a cookie sheet in small mounds spaced about 2″ apart.

9. Bake for about 30 minutes until dough puffs and turns golden brown.

10. Cut off the top third of the swans with a sharp knife. You may find some unbaked dough inside; remove this with your fingers, or with a teaspoon. (This keeps the puffs crisper and makes more room for filling.)

11. If you want your swans to spread their wings cut the removed top-third in two, lengthwise, to form wings.

12. To assemble the swans, whip the cream until it stands in soft peaks. Add the sugar and vanilla. Fill each swan with whipped cream.

13. Stick the necks in the filling at the right angle. Add more filling until it almost overflows. Place the wings over the filling and your swans are ready to sail to the table.

MOCK MARZIPAN FRUIT
(Photograph on page 56)

With your own hands mold beautiful little fruits that taste like expensive marzipan, but are made of simple materials that are readily available. The colorful fruits can be served as a sweet or dessert.

For About 30 Fruits
1 3-oz. pkg. of lemon flavored gelatin
2/3 cup sweetened condensed milk
1 cup ground coconut
1 cup ground oats
2 tbls. ground blanched almonds
1 tsp. almond extract
Food coloring (red, green, yellow)
Whole cloves

1. Grind the oats, coconut and almonds together. The finer they are ground, the better the 'marzipan' will be. (Try your blender for grinding.)

2. Put the gelatin in a medium bowl and add the condensed milk. Mix well until all the gelatin dissolves. Add the ground ingredients. Mix well and stir in extract; the mixture should look like 'play dough' for children. If it is too soft, add more ground almonds or coconut.

3. Divide the mixture into thirds. Add a different food coloring to each part. Make apples, pears, etc., from the green marzipan-dough. Bananas, lemons, etc., from the yellow. Strawberries, cherries, and other red fruits from the red.

4. To shape the fruits easily, grease your hands with salad oil and work with balls of dough 1″ in diameter. Accent the fruits with additional colors such as a blush of red to the apple. Add whole cloves as stems.

5. Dry the 'marzipan' fruits for about 2 hours in a chilled place, then store in an air tight box at room temperature. When sending as a gift frame each fruit in a small paper cup and arrange in a festive container.

SMILING CHOCOLATE CLOWNS
(Photograph on page 52)

These charming clowns are made of cookie crumbs and use ice cream cones as collars and hats. The designs shown give only a hint of the wide variety of expressions these funny fellows can assume.

For 6 Clowns
2½ cups vanilla wafer crumbs
8 oz. unsalted margarine (2 sticks)
6 oz. semi-sweet chocolate
3 tbls. strong black coffee
1 tsp. vanilla extract
1 tsp. rum extract

Decorating materials:
2 oz. semi-sweet chocolate
½ cup tiny chocolate candies
12 ice cream cones
¼ cup frosting (leftover from another cake)

1. Crush vanilla wafers and measure 2½ cups.

2. Melt 6 ounces chocolate with 3 tablespoons black coffee on top of a double boiler. When completely melted remove from heat and cool slightly.

3. Beat the margarine in a larger bowl until fluffy. Whip in the chocolate gradually, beating after each addition. Add the crumbs and the flavorings and mix well.

4. Chill until the mixture is manageable. Shape into 6 equal balls and put onto waxed paper. Chill thoroughly.

5. Melt 2 ounces chocolate with 2 tablespoons water in top of double boiler. Spread the tiny chocolate candies on a flat plate. Cut 6 ice cream cones 1½″ from the rim with a serrated knife. Use these as stands.

6. Dip each ball in the melted chocolate then roll in the candies to cover completely. Put on a 'stand.'

7. Invert another ice cream cone on top of each ball for a hat. Decorate each ball, giving it a happy face with leftover frosting. Decorate the hats with frosting, too, and attach colorful candies.

Animals From Yeast Dough

Our yeast cakes in animal disguise can be enjoyed with little formality. They can be eaten at breakfast instead of bread, or served with coffee for any occasion. They are light and even-textured with a rich golden color inside and a beautiful brown 'tan' outside. Pleasingly sweet, they still take nicely to some icing or a spreading of jam.

One recipe of Basic Yeast Dough (see index) is enough for four Frightful Crocodiles *or* four Friendly Turtles. You may, of course, mix and match these whimsical fragrant cakes to make your own private zoo.

THE FRIGHTFUL CROCODILE
(Photograph on page 56)

When you work with the yeast dough you will find it full of life. It shrinks, expands and changes its shape in front of your eyes. However, by following the instructions you will be able to take advantage of these qualities and get life-like crocodiles.

For 4 Crocodiles
1 recipe of Basic Yeast Dough (see index)
½ cup flour
4 tbls. milk
8 green chocolate candies, for eyes
1 tbls. Sugar-Glaze-Cement (see index)

1. Preheat the oven to 375°F. Lightly grease a cookie sheet. Have a pair of scissors handy.

2. Divide dough into 4 equal parts. Each part is enough for one crocodile. (The detailed in-structions given here are for one. Repeat the same procedures for the rest, or use part of the dough to make turtles.)

3. Divide the piece of dough into 3 equal parts. Two-thirds will serve as the body, the other one-third as the head and feet.

4. Dip your hands in flour. Roll the two-thirds of the dough in your hands to make a thin tail. Pull the thin end and pinch it to a point. The length of the body and tail should be 8″ to 8½″. Set aside on a floured surface.

5. Take the remaining dough and pinch off 2 pieces for the legs. Roll these between your hands until you have 2 thin 'ropes' 5″ long and ⅝″ thick. Place side by side on the cookie sheet about 4″ apart.

6. Fashion the head by rolling remaining dough between your hands. The head should be pointed and narrower than the body.

7. Put the body of the crocodile over the legs. If the body did shrink a little roll and pinch it back to its original shape.

8. Put the head on the cookie sheet and attach to the body by pinching together at the seam.

9. Brush the back of the crocodile with a little milk and let stand in a warm corner of the kitchen for half an hour.

10. Now make the scales, a most important part of the crocodile. You do it with floured scissors: Point tips toward head, handle toward tail; open the blades about 1″ then, starting just below the neck, stick scissors in the dough to a depth of about one-third of the thickness. Tilt the scissors backwards and snip. Make 4 rows, 2 or 3 scales per row. Make 2 cuts in each leg to create 3 fingers. (You can do this in less time than it takes to read the instructions.)

11. Bake for about 30 minutes. When the crocodile is nicely browned, remove from the oven.

12. Immediately cut the head to make the mouth. Support the mouth, in an open position, with a small cookie, or half a walnut.

13. After the crocodile is completely cool attach eyes with drop of Sugar-Glaze-Cement.

14. Repeat all steps with each quarter of remaining dough.

Attractive to look at and really quite easy to prepare.

For 4 Turtles

1 recipe Basic Yeast Dough (see index)
½ cup flour
4 tbls. milk

1. Preheat the oven to 375°F. Lightly grease a cookie sheet.

2. Divide the Basic Yeast Dough into 4 equal parts. Each part is enough for one turtle. (The detailed instructions given here are for one. Repeat the same procedures for the rest, or use part of the dough to make crocodiles.)

3. Divide the piece of dough into 4 parts. Three will serve as the body and the other for the head and legs.

4. Dust your hands in flour and form the 3 pieces of dough in an egg-shaped ball. Put on a floured surface.

5. Take the remaining dough and roll it between your hands to make a 'rope' ¾" thick.

6. Cut a piece 2" long for the head. Cut the rest in 2 equal parts for legs.

7. Place the legs side by side, about 2" apart, on the baking sheet. Put the body on top. Connect the head by pinching to the body.

8. Brush the top of the turtle with the milk. Let stand in a warm corner of the kitchen for about half an hour.

9. With a very sharp knife make cuts ¼" deep in the body: 2 lengthwise and 3 crosswise.

10. Bake for 30 minutes, until the turtle is nicely browned.

Animals From Store-Bought Cookies

Even if you do not have time to bake, you can still amaze your children and guests with animals made from store-bought cookies. In the picture you can see two frogs and two owls, for which we give instructions here.

Because these animals are three-dimensional it is difficult to explain the method of preparation in brief. So we suggest that you look at the picture very carefully when you decide to make them. We further suggest that you keep the book open, while you work for easier reference to the picture.

Important Note: Do not let the long and detailed explanation scare you. The preparation time is shorter than the time it takes to read the instructions.

THE JUMPING FROG
(Photograph on page 56)

For 1 Frog

2 round cookies, about 3" in diameter, for the back and mouth
1 round cookie, about 2" in diameter, for the tummy
2 round cookies, about 1½" in diameter, for the legs
2 chocolate drops, for the eyes
3 tsp. Sugar-Glaze-Cement (see index)

1. Spread a thin layer of 'cement' on the bottom of the 2" tummy cookie and attach it to the bottom of the 3" back cookie.

2. Place the second 3" cookie on a cutting board and cut off the top one-third with a serrated knife. Use sawing motion to avoid breaking the cookie. Hold the knife at an angle toward the top third of the cookie. (This angle cut will make the mouth appear open when attached to the body.)

3. Spread the cut part of the one-third cookie section with 'cement' and attach to the body cookie. Let dry for at least 10 minutes.

4. Now the most critical step in assembly: standing the frog on its own feet, put a teaspoon of 'cement' on top of each leg cookie, covering one-fourth of the area. Place the leg cookies side by side so that the 'cement' on each touches.

5. Set the body on its feet, tilting slightly forward. Support at front with a cup, or lean against the wall. Unhand very carefully. If the leg cookies are too slippery put them on a paper towel.

6. Should the frog fall apart do not give up. Add more 'cement' and stand the frog a little more vertically. You have to replace the 'cement', however, since once it dries and breaks it will not hold.

7. Let the frog dry for *at least* an hour without touching or testing.

8. After the frog dries, attach the eyes with two drops of 'cement'.

THE WISE OWL
(Photograph on page 56)

For 1 Owl

1 elongated cookie, about 4″ long and 2½″ wide, for the body
1 round cookie, about 2″ in diameter, for the tummy
2 round cookies, about 1½″ in diameter, for the legs
2 thin round flat candies, about ¾″ in diameter, for the eyes
4 chocolate drops, for the pupils and ears
3 tsp. Sugar-Glaze-Cement (see index)

1. Spread a thin layer of 'cement' on the bottom of the tummy cookie and attach it to the bottom of the body cookie.

2. Spread a thin layer of 'cement' on the thin round candies. Glue them to the body so they touch each other and extend over the edge of the body. Let dry for 10 minutes.

3. Proper standing of the owl on its legs is the key to its appearance. Put a teaspoon of 'cement' on top of each leg cookie, covering one-fourth of the area. Place side by side so that the 'cement' on both of them touches.

4. Put the owl's body, leaning forward at a slight angle, over the legs. Support it against the wall or with a cup. Let dry for *at least* an hour without touching.

5. Once the connection to the legs is dry and firm, 'cement' on the chocolate ears.

6. The location of the pupils will determine the character of the owl. It can be cock-eyed, amazed, or watching wisely according to the way its pupils are placed. Try a number of possibilities before you decide on the final location of the pupils. Glue them on with a dab of 'cement'.

7. After you finish one owl you will find it impossible to resist making more and more.

Animals From Taffy-Candy

Taffy is a material that lends itself to molding and shaping very easily. In our picture we used dark taffies for the Busy Bees and light for the Small Turtles. In our experiments we found that the behavior of taffy can vary from one batch to the next. So experiment with your taffy before starting your 'assembly line' operation. Once you are familiar with the behavior of your taffy under heat and with moisture, the preparation is very quick indeed.

THE SMALL TURTLES
(Photograph on page 56)

The ease with which taffy can be shaped when softened under heat, is the secret in making these turtles.

For 1 Turtle

1 large light brown taffy, for the body
4 pecan halves, for the legs
1 pecan quarter, for the head

1. Preheat the oven to 325°F.

2. Place the leg and head nuts on a cookie sheet and put the taffy on top.

3. Put in the oven for a short time: 4 to 8 minutes. The taffy should soften, but not melt completely.

4. Remove from oven. Press the taffy onto the nuts, with a lightly oiled wide knife. Work quickly.

5. Cool a little, remove from the cookie sheet and put on waxed paper. The turtles are ready when they are cool and the nuts are firmly attached to the taffy.

6. If one taffy is not enough add a second one to top of the turtle and return to the oven. Remove and press the second taffy until it is welded to the first.

THE BUSY BEES
(Photograph on page 56)

Our taffy bees have legs and antennae of dark waxed paper to make them quite natural looking. Get your dark waxed paper from candy bar wrappers and linings of candy boxes.

For 1 Bee

1 dark taffy, for the body
2 perfect almonds of equal size, for the wings
1 piece of dark waxed paper, for the legs and antennae

1. Trace the drawing of the legs and antennae on a piece of transparent paper. Fold the dark

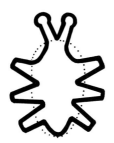

waxed paper over itself to the approximate size of the drawing, which allows you to make many sets with one cut.

2. Warm the taffy slightly by rolling it between your hands, dipping briefly in warm water, or placing over a very low heat. Shape in an elongated oval.

3. Wet the taffy to make it sticky, and place over the legs.

4. Hold the 2 almonds in both hands and at one time stick them to the body of the bee, about one-third from the head.

5. Let cool and dry.

6. Once you prepare one bee you will realize that it is quicker to make them than to read these instructions. You will want to make many more bees, and arrange them in an attractive 'formation' on the serving dish.

POPPED CORN KING
(Photograph on page 56)

The impressive looking king in our picture can be made in a few minutes, and yet is cute, tasty and full of humorous *Purim-Spirit*.

For 1 'King'

Body:
4 cups popped corn (2 oz.)
15 taffy candy (caramel)
2 tbls. water

Decorations:
2 green chocolate candies, for the eyes
1 red chocolate candy, for the nose
2 Hamantashen, for shoes
1 empty paper cup, for the crown
1 yellow pipe cleaner, for the scepter

1. In the top of a double boiler put the taffies and water. Heat, stirring, until the taffies melt and become a sticky syrup.

2. Put the popped corn in a large bowl. Pour the syrup over and toss to coat evenly.

3. Wet your hands and make balls, pressing the corn firmly.

4. Attach 2 balls, as illustrated, while they are still sticky. (Use 2 per king or snowman.)

5. Apply the decorations in the proper locations with drops of syrup. Feel free to improvise and improve on our design.

Build your own Storyland Castle, as a centerpiece for Purim celebration or any other happy occasion. The ingredients are delicious: cake, candies, ice cream cones and sugar wafers. All the brave guards have a heart of . . . chocolate, and will not prevent anyone from enjoying the sweet MAGIC CASTLE (recipes start on next page).

The Magic Castle

(Photographs on page 64)

This colorful confection can be King Ahasuerus' Persian Palace if you wish or it can be an exotic mansion right out of The Thousand and One Nights. Whatever theme you choose the Magic Castle will bring lots of fun and pleasure. In addition to being handsome it is very tasty because its building blocks are sponge cakes, its plaster sweet frostings and the ornaments candies, cookies and other goodies.

The Magic Castle is suitable for any occasion when several cakes might be needed, especially if guests are members of the young set. Besides being an entire party menu all in one, it allows you to build your party around a central theme. That way you can tell a story instead of just serving sweets and cakes.

Wonderful for birthday parties, remember the Magic Castle when you need a 'spectacular' for school affairs or fund-raising projects. Select a theme, let your imagination go and place this delightful palace in a storyland of your own.

It is highly recommended that the construction of the castle be done over a period of several days. It is almost impossible to prepare everything in one day. Building the castle at home includes a visit to the nearby candy counter for decorating materials, baking the cakes, preparing a large amount of frosting and last, but not least, the assembly.

BASIC SPONGE CAKE

This cake is also called *Lekach* and is the number one cake of the Jewish kitchen. It is so light and delicate in texture that its looks alone make you feel good. The inside is bright yellow, like a child's painting of the sun, and the crust is a golden brown. Subtly flavored with vanilla and fresh lemon, the fragrance makes you ask for more. *Lekach* is the right choice for any occasion, especially holidays and entertaining; and is also perfect for cake sculpturing.

For 10" Tube Cake, or 9" x 13" x 2" Flat Cake, or
9" x 3" Round Cake, or 2 9" x 1½" Round Cakes

8 extra large eggs at room temperature
1½ cups sugar
4 tbls. water
1 tsp. grated lemon rind
1 tsp. vanilla extract
1½ cups flour, sifted before measuring
¼ tsp. salt
1½ tsp. baking powder

1. Preheat the oven to 350°F. Lightly oil and flour baking utensil.

2. Separate the eggs; put the yolks in a large mixing bowl and the whites in a very large mixing bowl.

3. Sift the flour with the salt and baking powder.

4. Beat the egg yolks, gradually adding half of the sugar. Add the water, lemon rind and vanilla extract; continue beating until the yolks become thick and lemon-colored.

5. Fold in the dry ingredients very gently and gradually until a very smooth, lump free batter is obtained.

6. Clean and dry the beaters. Whip the egg whites until they are foamy. Add the sugar, 1 tablespoon after the other, whipping after each addition. The whipped egg whites should hold their shape and look soft and glossy.

7. Fold one-fourth of the whipped egg whites very gently into the yolk mixture. When blended fold into another one-fourth very gently. Now, transfer the fluffy yolk mixture into the whipped egg whites and combine the two with wide folding movements, using a spatula or a big spoon. Batter is ready when no white streaks remain.

8. Pour the batter into lightly greased baking pan or pans. Bake until an inserted toothpick comes out dry and clean. Allow about 45 minutes to large cakes, 30 minutes to shallow ones. (Specific baking times are given with other cakes.)

9. When the cakes are done, remove from oven and cool partially. Remove from pans and cool completely on racks.

BASE AND TERRACE OF THE MANSION

1 recipe Basic Sponge Cake (see above)
1 8″ springform pan, for base
1 10″ springform pan, for terrace

1. Make cake as directed, distributing batter as follows: pour two-thirds into the 8″ springform pan and one-third into the 10″ pan.

2. Bake the 10″ pan 30 to 35 minutes, the 8″ pan 30 to 45 minutes. (Cakes are done when a toothpick comes out clean.)

Note: both pans may be baked at one time. Just be sure there is enough space in the oven to allow free circulation of heat.

DOMES OF THE CASTLE

1 recipe Basic Sponge Cake (see above)
1½ quart oven-proof bowl, for mansion dome
2 6-oz. oven-proof cups, for tower domes
2 10-oz. oven-proof cups, for tower domes

1. Make cake as directed, distributing batter as follows: fill the big bowl to 1″ from rim; fill the smaller cups to ¼″ from rim. (Bake one more cupcake for your own enjoyment if there is any left-over batter.)

2. Bake the 6-ounce cakes 12 to 15 minutes; 10-ounce cakes 15 to 18 minutes and the big bowl 30 to 35 minutes. Test for doneness with a toothpick.

3. Cool partially, run a thin spatula around edges of baking utensils to ease cakes out. Cool on racks.

Note: cakes may be baked at one time. Just be sure there is enough space in the oven to allow free circulation of heat.

FROSTINGS FOR THE CASTLE MANSION

Coating the Mansion cakes with frosting is a crucial step in the creation of the Magic Castle. Prepare a basic frosting first then divide it in three parts and color each one differently.

8 oz. unsalted margarine (2 sticks)
2 lb. confectioners' sugar
½ cup cold water
2 eggs
2 tsp. vanilla extract
Food coloring: red, yellow, blue

1. Take the margarine out of the refrigerator about 30 minutes before you start preparing the frosting.

2. Sift the sugar into a large bowl. The sifting prevents lumps, and helps assure a smooth, homogeneous frosting.

3. Whip the softened margarine in another bowl with an electric mixer or a good hand beater. Whip until fluffy. Gradually add the sifted confectioners' sugar. From time to time add ½ tablespoon cold water which makes the mixture more manageable. When about half of the sugar is combined, add the eggs and vanilla extract. Add the remaining sugar and water and beat well.

4. Divide the frosting into 3 equal parts, placing each part into a small bowl. Add a few drops of the red food coloring to one bowl, and mix well. If you want a deeper color add another drop and mix. Repeat the same with the other colors.

5. At this stage the frosting will tend to be too soft for further work. Put it in the refrigerator for about 30 minutes.

CONSTRUCTION AND DECORATION OF THE MANSION

Careful construction and decoration will make your mansion a feast to the eyes. We used sweets, cookies and candies in a variety of shapes and textures to give the castle in our picture an 'Oriental' look. You can, of course, use your own imagination and vary our design.

For Constructing And Decorating The Mansion
The Base Cake
The Terrace Cake
The Dome Cake
Colored frostings
Sugar-Glaze-Cement (see index)

Decorating materials for the Base:
120 brown chocolate candies
10 semi-circle cookies
10 gate-shaped cookies

Decorating materials for the Terrace:
12 semi-circle marmalades in assorted colors

Decorating materials for the Dome:
16 orange chocolate candies
9 yellow chocolate candies
8 brown chocolate candies
24 green chocolate candies
60 red chocolate candies
8 semi-circle cookies

1. Coat each cake with a thin layer of frosting of the appropriate color. This thin layer will hold down the crumbs, making it easier to assemble and apply the final coating.

2. Place the Base cake on a flat plate, or a bottom of a springform. (Putting the cake on a flat surface will make it easier to place it later on the 'castle ground.') Coat the Base with a second layer of the blue frosting.

3. Place the Terrace cake on the center of the Base cake and coat it with a second layer of the pink frosting.

4. Put the Dome cake on the center of the Terrace cake very carefully. When you apply the second coating of the yellow frosting to the Dome you will find that it is rather difficult to achieve a smooth, even surface. Use a fork to make grooves on the Dome forming a repeated pattern. (The cookies and candies that go on later will also help to achieve an even surface. The red chocolate candies around the baseline of the Dome will cover imperfections in that region.)

5. To decorate the Mansion follow the list of ingredients, and look at the picture as you go. Attach the cookies and candies to the cakes by pressing them gently into the frosting. Be careful and precise in locating the decorations; be sure that the lines and angles are equal and symmetrical.

CONSTRUCTION OF THE TOWERS

The castle is surrounded by six towers: two Tall Observation Towers, two Guarding Towers, and two Gate Towers. The major building material for the Towers are round doughnuts stacked vertically and supported by long pencils or knitting pins taped together. You also need Sugar-Glaze-Cement for 'gluing' and decorating the Towers.

The Tall Observation Towers

2 6-oz. cupcakes, for the domes (see above)
1 10-oz. cupcakes, for the domes (see above)
12 large doughnuts (3" in diameter, 1½" thick)
2 hard sweet-sour candies, for the top
12 yellow chocolate candies
Sugar-Glaze-Cement (see index)
2 paper flags

1. Stack 6 doughnuts for each tower. Stabilize the towers as recommended above or find another solution. Move them as little as possible.

2. Place the cupcakes on top of the towers as shown in picture. Again, do try to support them by sticking something through them to prevent toppling.

3. Decorate in Oriental design with Sugar-Glaze-Cement. Use a drop of this 'cement' to glue on the yellow chocolate candies.

4. Top each tower with a hard sweet-sour candy. You can wet it with a drop of water to make it shine brilliantly.

5. Stick the poles of the flags into the cakes, just behind the shining candy.

The Guarding Towers

14 small doughnuts, dipped in confectioners' sugar
2 sugar ice cream cones
2 small marmalade squares
2 paper flags

1. Stack 7 small doughnuts around a pencil. The reduced height improves the stability considerably and these towers are much easier to handle.

2. Place a sugar cone on top of each tower. Attach the small marmalade squares to the tips of the cones by pressing with your finger.

3. Stick the poles of the flags through the marmalade squares into the tips of the cones.

The Gate Towers

8 small doughnuts
2 sugar ice cream cones
2 small marmalade squares
2 paper flags

1. Follow the same instruction as for Guarding Towers, but this time build each Tower only four doughnuts high.

CONSTRUCTION OF THE PROTECTING WALLS AND DRAW BRIDGE

Fearsome Protecting Walls guard the privacy of our Magic Castle with sweet sugar wafers. We suggest building them like real brick walls which will make them stable and amazingly strong.

11 2½-oz. pkg. sugar wafers 3½"x¾"x¼" (about 130)
20 wooden toothpicks
Sugar-Glaze-Cement

1. The protecting walls are constructed of 6 segments: four short, and 2 long. All the seg-

ments are 10 wafer thicknesses high and topped with 'teeth' 2 wafer thicknesses high. Use the Sugar-Glaze-Cement to connect the wafers, and occasionally insert a wooden toothpick vertically into the walls to help hold everything together.

2. *The four short segments:* These segments are 1 wafer long. Place 1 wafer on the table and put 2 drops of the Sugar-Glaze-Cement about 1" from its tips. Cut a second wafer in half and place the halves, slightly separated from each other, on top of the first wafer. Put a drop of 'cement' on each half and place a whole wafer on top. Continue until you get the full height.

3. *The two long segments:* These segments are 2 wafers long and here a brick wall structure is really essential to keep everything together. Place 2 wafers end to end on the table. Glue a whole wafer, half over each of the 2 wafers, with 2 drops of the Sugar-Glaze-Cement. Glue 2 wafer halves on each end to complete the second layer. The third layer is exactly like the first one. The fourth is like the second, etc. Continue until you get the full height.

4. *The 'teeth':* We place 5 'teeth' on the long segments and 3 on the short ones. Thus we have a total of 22 'teeth'. Each tooth is 2 wafer-thicknesses high. From 2 wafers you can make 4 'teeth'. However, since the wafers are very brittle we recommend that you prepare the 'teeth' one by one. First cut the 2 wafers one on top of the other, then glue the tooth and immediately glue it in place.

5. *The draw bridge:* To complete the defense system of the castle make a draw bridge from 4 wafers. Connect them, side to side, with a small amount of Sugar-Glaze-Cement.

FINAL ASSEMBLY OF THE MAGIC CASTLE

In addition to the components you have prepared to this point you will need the following to give the castle its final touches:

> Corrugated cardboard, 24" x 22"
> White waxed freezer paper
> Piece of red ribbon
> 10 chocolate soldiers
> Lightweight cardboard or heavy paper, cut in strips 1½" x ½"

1. Select a piece of cardboard strong enough to support the Castle. Cut it according to the draw-

ing. Cover with white paper to resist stains from doughnuts and frosting.

2. If you plan to transport the Magic Castle we strongly recommend that it be assembled at the final destination. (Carry the components separately, all individually wrapped and well-protected.) Even at home you should assemble the castle on the spot where it will be viewed before cutting.

3. Follow the drawing and picture to make sure you locate the parts correctly. Place the Mansion at center rear of the cardboard base, with 2 Short Wall Segments on either side. Add the Tall Observation Towers very carefully. Put the 2 Long Wall Segments near them. Butt the Guard Towers into these walls. From these towers 2 more Short Walls lead to the Gate Towers. Put Draw Bridge in place and connect it, with a piece of red ribbon, just under the sugar cones, to the tops of Gate Towers.

4. Cover the floor of the castle yard with crackers to resemble marble tiles.

5. Fold strips of lightweight cardboard in half lengthwise and attach to backs of chocolate soldiers with tape or Sugar-Glaze-Cement. Place soldiers around castle as indicated. It is best to tuck the free part of each soldier's support under a cracker to make sure he stands at attention at his post.

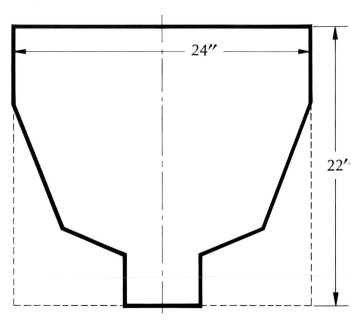

VII

PASSOVER: FREEDOM AND SPRINGTIME FARE

PASSOVER IS CELEBRATED in spring and in Israel the sweet scent of new blossoms always perfumes the air. The holiday commemorates the Jewish escape from slavery in ancient Egypt to freedom in the Land of Israel. Springtime and nature's rebirth seem to reinforce the main theme of Passover: liberation from oppression and a return to a life of dignity. The origins of the holiday may be ancient, but the season and spirit of the holiday have never grown old. Both evoke cheerful feelings of renewal and optimism, thereby making Passover a very special, very beautiful milestone on the Hebrew calendar.

The Exodus occurred about four-thousand years ago when the Israelites escaped the tyranny of the Pharaohs under the leadership of Moses. Passover starts on the Fourteenth day of the Hebrew month of *Nisan,* the same day the Jews fled from Egypt. The holiday opens with the *Seder* ceremony and lasts seven days.

During Passover leavened bread is not allowed. This custom is directly related to the Exodus. In the rush there was no time to leaven bread so a mixture of flour and water was baked and created a new kind of bread, the *Matzah.* This special thin, crisp 'cake' is eaten throughout the holiday instead of bread, till this very day.

As a result of this dietary law many strict regulations apply to eating and cooking. Flour and leavened-flour products such as noodles, rolls and regular cakes are strictly forbidden during the entire holiday. To be sure there is no trace of bread in the house the period just before Passover for many people is one of hectic preparations. The home is completely cleaned and scrubbed with special attention given to the kitchen to assure that not even the tiniest bread crumb remains hidden in a forgotten drawer. Even utensils are exchanged for special Passover ones. It is no wonder, then, that the house is sparkling clean just in time for the *Seder* ceremony.

The *Seder* Ceremony

The *Seder* marks the beginning of Passover and is one of the major events of the Jewish year. It is a unique evening that combines religious ceremony with a festive meal and takes place at home, with the entire family in attendance. *Seder* means 'Order' in Hebrew; and indeed the *Seder* proceeds in order according to details fixed by law and custom. A special prayer book, the *Haggadah,* is read during the evening. This

Clockwise, from the top there are: CHOCOLATE MOUSSE, garnished with whipped cream rossettes (recipe on page 86), UPSIDE-DOWN, NON-BAKE FRUIT CAKE (recipe on page 74), CHOCOLATE MATZO ROLL (recipe on page 80), MERINGUE SHELLS (recipe on page 85) filled with whipped cream, strawberries, and garnished with mint leaves, and a FRUIT PIE—KOSHER LE'PESSACH (recipe on page 77). In the center are tiny NUT BONBONS (recipe on page 90). In the background is the Haggadah, the book that contains the instructions for carrying on the ceremony of welcoming Passover.

book contains instructions for carrying out the *Seder*, for benedictions to be said, for songs to be sung, and for *Kushiot*, questions to be asked by youngsters; as well as the answers to be given to the children by the adults.

The *Seder* table is set with the most beautiful tablecloth, dishes and wine goblets. Candles, flowers and fruits decorate the table to create a distinctive holiday atmosphere. Symbolic foods of Passover are put on the table to be explained throughout the ceremony. They include three *matzot*, individually wrapped and placed one over the other, and a Passover plate set near the head of the family. This plate contains a shankbone, *Zeroa*, to represent the Paschal Lamb sacrifice in ancient times; a hard boiled egg, to express grief for the destruction of the Temple; bitter herbs, *Maror*, prepared from horseradish, to recall the bitterness of slavery; *Haroset*, a mixture of nuts, apples and wine to resemble the clay and bricks the Jews had to make in Egypt; and sprigs of parsley or celery to symbolize spring, life, and hope by their fresh green color.

Other traditional items for the *Seder* are bowls of salted water to recall the tears shed in Egypt: they are used for dipping the green parsley. A second dipping ritual occurs during the *Seder*: *Maror* is dipped in the *Haroset*, and eaten by all.

But the *Seder* is not just serious business, it is fun as well. A delicious dinner is served, that features foods tradition has preserved and generations have improved. Wine is poured to fill each participant's cup four times during the ceremony and the mood gets better and better. There is one cup of wine on the table, however, that no one is allowed to touch. This is Elijah's cup and is usually a beautifully ornamented vessel of gold or silver. The children attending the *Seder* expect Elijah the Prophet to come in at any minute to drink from his cup; this keeps them awake, sometimes until the end of the ceremony.

Another way to keep youngsters awake and alert is the *Afikoman*. The *Afikoman* is a piece of *Matzah* taken from the second of the three wrapped *Matzot*. The father tucks it away to be eaten at the very end of the meal. The children, in turn, try to steal the *Afikoman* and hide it somewhere else. They agree to return it only if they are promised a nice present. After some negotiations, the presents are promised, the *Afikoman* is returned and the meal ends. The *Seder* comes to its conclusion after further reading in the *Haggadah*. The grand finale is the singing of Passover songs in good humor and high spirits until the small hours of the night.

Children love Passover as much as their parents and grandparents do, or even more so. The youngsters take part in the preparations before the holiday, they are happy with their new clothes and shoes, and they have fun playing with an assortment of filberts, walnuts and other nuts. Children look forward to the *Seder* not only for the presents to be promised in return for the *Afikoman*, but also because they enjoy the coziness of the family seated around the festive table praying, eating and singing together. There is no generation gap at the *Seder* ceremony.

Planning a Successful *Seder*

Two *Seder* dinners complete with menus, detailed recipes and tips for planning and cooking are included in this chapter. The menus are composed of traditional dishes mainly, with some new ones. Several dishes can be prepared a day before the *Seder*. Take advantage of this and do as much as you can in advance.

In addition to the complete menu you will need hard-boiled eggs for all of the guests, bowls of salted water, and the Passover plate with the symbolic foods (recipe for *Haroset* follows). Don't forget to have enough wine in reserve to provide four cups for each guest.

We highly recommend that you make it easy on yourself by enlisting the help of your husband and children. They can be responsible for getting the accessories like *yarmulkas* (skull caps), *Haggadah* books, extra chairs, and to wheel in a comfortable armchair for the head of the family who conducts the ceremony. He is referred to as the 'King of the *Seder*' and is supposed to recline on a cushioned 'throne'. With these jobs taken care of, you can have a good rest before the ceremony. A smiling hostess assures the success of the *Seder*.

A Savory *Seder* Menu

The menu of this dinner is basically the same as that served by Jewish mothers for generations. But we dared to introduce some minor changes of our own, taking into account modern tastes and diet-consciousness. As a first course we serve Artichokes with a Creamy Sauce. Artichokes are typical spring vegetables and we feel that they should adorn the festive table of Passover, the holiday of spring. This course can be made well in advance, even the day before, since it is served cold. We proceed to soup with delicate *Chremslach* (one of Passover's soup dumplings). To us, clear soup with the traditional holiday dumplings in it is a pillar of a festive meal and we could not do without it.

The main course is a Savory Brisket roasted slowly in the oven. This is a relatively inexpensive dish, but after marinating and proper roasting it becomes very tender and flavorful. We take advantage of the heated oven to bake a Potato *Kugel*. The *Kugel* should be put in the oven about two hours before serving time. Glazed Beets are added to provide tartness and color. The beets, too, can be prepared ahead and reheated. Our dessert is modern, light and fruity. We called it Upside-Down, Non-Bake Fruit Cake. Serve it with *demi-tasse* or tea.

MENU
(planned for 6 to 8)
Artichokes with Creamy Sauce*
Chremslach (Passover soup dumplings),*
in clear soup
Savory Brisket*
Potato Kugel*
Glazed Beets*
Tossed green salad
Upside-Down, Non-Bake Fruit Cake*
Demi-Tasse or Tea
Recipe given

HAROSET

There are many versions of *Haroset*, the sweet 'clay' that is eaten during the *Seder* ceremony. But the principle is quite simple: mix together nuts, fruits, wine and spices, such as cinnamon. You, too, may create your own version.

½ cup ground nuts
1 big apple
2 tbls. sweet wine
1 tsp. sugar
½ tsp. cinnamon

1. Grate the apple and add the rest of the ingredients. Mix well.

ARTICHOKES WITH CREAMY SAUCE

Artichokes are a very striking and delicious vegetable. When placed on individual plates to be served as first course, they look like flowers and actually decorate the table. Put creamy sauce in small individual sauce plates and direct your guests to dip the leaves in it.

One Artichoke Per Person
6-8 medium artichokes
8 cups water
1 tbls. salt
2 tbls. oil
2 tbls. lemon juice
1 tbls. snipped parsley

Creamy sauce:
12 oz. mayonnaise (1½ cups)
4 tbls. lemon juice
3 tbls. snipped parsley
1 garlic clove, mashed

1. Choose medium-sized artichokes of bright, green color with leaves tightly closed. Use a big pot, preferably of stainless-steel, for cooking.

2. Prepare the artichokes: remove the stems and cut ½" off the tips of the leaves with scissors. Rub all the cut places with lemon juice to prevent discoloration.

3. Arrange the artichokes in the big pot, putting them in an upright position, very close to one another. This helps keep their shape. Cover the artichokes with the water (add more, if necessary, to cover completely). Add the salt, oil and lemon juice. Cover the pot and cook for 30 to 40 minutes, until an inside leaf may be pulled off easily.

4. Remove the artichokes from the pot and turn them upside down in a colander, for about 15 minutes or until all the water has drained off.

5. After the artichokes cool open the center of each very gently with your fingers. Remove some of the center leaves to form a cup. Now that the opening is broader remove the 'chokes', the inedible fuzzy part, with a teaspoon or grapefruit knife.

6. Prepare the sauce by mixing ingredients together. You can do this ahead of time and keep it in the refrigerator. Stir again just before serving. Put the sauce in very small dishes to be placed near each person.

7. To serve the artichokes, stand each upright on a salad plate. You may have to spread some of the bottom leaves to support the artichokes in a standing position.

CHREMSLACH

Chremslach are soup dumplings that resemble small, puffed pancakes, and are served in a clear chicken broth or bouillon. They are so light they float, yet are crisp and crunchy. Plan on serving two or three *chremslach* in each soup plate.

For About 20 Chremslach
2 eggs, separated
¼ cup matzo meal
2 tbls. potato starch
½ tsp. salt
Dash black pepper
Oil for frying

1. Whip the egg whites with the salt until they hold their shape and stand in soft peaks. Add the yolks and mix in gently.

2. Measure the *matzo meal* and potato starch; add to the eggs. Fold gently so the volume of the whipped eggs does not diminish.

3. Put oil at least ½" deep in a large frying pan. Heat the oil and drop in the batter from a teaspoon. Fry on both sides until golden brown. Drain on paper towels or napkins. Serve warm in soup.

SAVORY BRISKET

A well prepared piece of brisket can be a very tasty dish. The secrets of the preparation are the marinating and the long, slow cooking. The recipe here calls for marinating the brisket overnight, then roasting it for about four hours.

5 lb. piece of brisket
1/3 cup lemon juice
1 cup red dry wine
¼ cup oil
2 tsp. salt
2 onions
6 garlic cloves
1 carrot
1 tsp. sugar
½ tsp. pepper

1. Make marinade: peel the vegetables; chop onions and garlic; and slice the carrot thinly. Put in a medium bowl and add lemon juice, wine, oil, salt, pepper, and sugar. Mix well.

2. Set the meat in a shallow roasting pan that will hold it comfortably, and pour on it all the marinade. Turn the meat until it is coated with the marinade on all sides.

3. Cover the pan with aluminum foil and put in refrigerator overnight. You can do this the evening before or the morning of dinner day. Turn the meat occasionaly so it will absorb the flavors on all sides.

4. Five hours before serving time put the meat in a 350°F oven. Be sure that the foil lid is secured tightly around the pan. When meat is covered while roasting, it does not dry out and retains the juices.

5. Roast for 4 to 4½ hours until meat is fork tender. Remove to a heated serving plate, and let it rest out of the oven until serving time, for easier slicing. Trim off some of the fat.

6. Skim the fat off pan juices, then reheat to pass around as a delicious sauce.

7. Slice the meat crosswise. Do it in the kitchen for easier serving.

POTATO KUGEL

Kugel is made of grated potatoes baked in the oven until they are tender, crisp and beautifully browned. It is an excellent companion to the Savory Brisket that can be made in the same oven at the same time.

2 lb. potatoes
1 medium onion
1 big carrot
¼ cup matzo meal
1 tsp. salt
⅛ tsp. pepper
2 eggs
3 tbls. oil or chicken fat

1. Peel the vegetables, cut in small pieces and put through a meat grinder. You can also grate them, in which case you don't have to cut them in small pieces.

2. Add the eggs, *matzo meal,* salt, pepper, and fat to the ground or grated vegetables. Mix well.

3. Grease a 9″ x 5″ x 2″ baking dish thoroughly. Put the mixture in and bake, uncovered, for 90 minutes at 350°F. The *kugel* is done when nicely browned and its edges look crisp.

4. Prepare the *kugel* to be ready before serving. If you make it some hours in advance keep it in a very slow oven.

GLAZED BEETS

Colorful and tasty, the beets are our second vegetable selection. They can be prepared ahead and reheated.

2 lb. small beets
2 tbls. salad oil
1 scant tbls. potato starch
1 tsp. salt
1/3 cup sugar
Dash pepper
2 tbls. lemon juice

1. Peel the beets and cook in water to cover until tender: about 30 minutes. Drain, saving one cup of liquid for the glaze.

2. Cool slightly and slice the beets ⅛″ thick, making even slices.

3. Combine the reserved beet liquid, sugar, salt, pepper, salad oil and lemon juice in a saucepan. Bring to a boil.

4. Mix the potato starch with 2 tablespoons water. Pour into boiling liquid, stirring constantly. Boil on reduced heat for 2 minutes. Add the sliced beets and cook for 2 minutes more. Serve immediately, or cool and reheat when needed.

UPSIDE-DOWN, NON-BAKE FRUIT CAKE
(Photograph on page 70)

You will not have to bake this beautiful upside-down cake. The top is a molded fruit dessert and the bottom supporting it is a layer of *matzo-*crumbs. The fruity top is made of flavored apple purée, apricots, cherries and mint leaves for garnish. Together they create a light, juicy and refreshing cake that can be served as a dessert.

2½ lb. tart apples
1 cup water
1 cup sugar
2 tbls. lemon juice
1 tbls. unflavored gelatin
2 tbls. brandy or fruit liqueur
7 canned cherries
1 1-lb. can apricot halves
Mint leaves
4 matzot, unsalted
2 oz. softened margarine (½ stick)

1. Peel the apples, core and slice thinly.

2. Bring the water, sugar and lemon juice to a boil in a big saucepan. Add the apples and cook on medium heat for 30 minutes, until the apples are tender and almost transparent looking. Stir occasionally.

3. Soften gelatin in ¼ cup water. Add to the apples and stir gently until completely dissolved. Remove from heat.

4. Add the brandy. Cool the apples until half set.

5. Line bottom and sides of an 8″ springform pan with 2 layers of waxed paper, or grease them lightly with a little oil. Drain the apricots, reserving ½ cup of the syrup. Drain the cherries also, and place the fruit on paper towels to absorb extra moisture.

6. Arrange 6 cherries in the bottom of the pan and cover each with an apricot half, to form a round garland (see picture). Put the apples above the apricots in the pan. Press lightly with the back of a tablespoon to distribute evenly.

7. Break the *matzot* into small pieces and moisten with the apricot syrup. Melt the margarine and pour over the pieces. Mix well, cover the apple layer with them. Cover the pan with waxed paper and refrigerate for 6 hours or overnight.

8. Before serving, run a knife around the edges of the pan. Invert on a cake platter and release the springform. Remove the sides and bottom. Lift off the waxed paper to discover the beautiful top. Add the last cherry to the center of the cake. Garnish with mint leaves and serve cold. At a dairy meal, you can add whipped cream to each slice.

A Delectable *Seder* Dinner

This menu features a Roast Turkey as the main course. The turkey requires some preparations several hours before the *Seder*, but, once in the oven, you don't have to worry about it until carving time. The Giblet Stuffing, which makes good use of giblets that might otherwise be wasted, is served as the starchy side dish, and cooks while the turkey roasts. The portions of the stuffing may seem small, but considering all of the other dishes offered, no one will leave the table hungry.

The first course is Chopped Liver, and you can't avoid eating crisp *matzah* with it. Soup, served with Airy *Kneidlach (matzo balls)* comes next. We suggest making the *kneidlach* tiny since they tend to be filling even when small. For your convenience, the chopped liver, soup and *Kneidlach* can be prepared well in advance. Other side dishes for the turkey are braised celery, delicately dressed in a sweet-and-sour sauce; and sliced, fresh tomatoes sprinkled with salt, pepper and a few drops of oil and lemon juice. To end the dinner on a sweet note we suggest a Fruit Pie, *Kosher Le'Pessach*, of course. As you can see, most of the dinner can be prepared ahead to enable you to rest some before the *Seder*.

M E N U
(planned for 6 to 8)
Chopped Liver*
Airy Kneidlach—Light Matzo Balls,*
  with clear soup
Roast Turkey* with
Giblet Stuffing*
Sweet and Sour Celery*
Sliced tomatoes
Fruit Pie—Kosher Le'Pessach*
Recipe given

CHOPPED LIVER

A very famous Jewish dish that can be eaten on Passover as a very appetizing and promising first course. You will find that chopped liver tastes even better when eaten with crisp *matzah*.

> 1½ lb. chicken liver
> 3 big onions
> 3 tbls. oil or chicken fat
> 1 tsp. salt
> ⅛ tsp. pepper
> 3 hard-boiled eggs

1. Broil the livers under hot broiler for about 7 minutes on each side. There should be no trace of blood.

2. Chop the onions and brown them in the oil or chicken fat until just golden. Don't let them get too brown or they will turn bitter.

3. Put the livers, onions and eggs through the finest blade of a meat grinder. Add salt and pepper. For a very smooth texture grind twice or use the blender. If you prefer a coarse texture, where the eggs, onions and liver are identifiable, chop with a knife on a bread board.

4. To serve, arrange nicely on a green lettuce leaf.

AIRY KNEIDLACH—LIGHT MATZO-BALLS

We call these little tasty Passover dumplings 'airy' because they are so delicate and light they actually float in clear hot chicken soup.

For About 24 Kneidlach

> 3 eggs
> 1¼ cups matzo meal
> 1 tsp. salt
> ½ cup chicken soup
> 3 tbls. chicken fat

1. Mix all ingredients well. Chill in refrigerator for 2 hours. During that time the mixture will set and become manageable after liquids are absorbed.

2. Bring a big pot of salted water to a boil. Moisten your hands with water and make small balls, 1″ in diameter. Drop balls in the boiling water and cook for about 30 minutes. Drain. Serve in very hot soup. You may reheat the *kneidlach* in the soup if you prepare both ahead of time.

ROAST TURKEY

A whole roast turkey is always fitting for a festive meal. Read the recipe and plan the preparation so it will be ready before the *Seder* starts. If you use a frozen turkey it should be completely thawed before roasting.

> 1 whole 8-10 lb. turkey
> 2 oz. margarine (½ stick)
> 2 tsp. salt
> ¼ tsp. pepper

1. Preheat oven to 450°F.

2. Rub the bird inside and out with salt and pepper. Stuff with the giblet stuffing and sew or skewer the opening. Place on its back on a large piece of aluminum foil. Brush with melted margarine. Fold the foil to cover the bird. Fold up ends to keep juice in. Place in a shallow open roasting pan.

3. Roast for 1¾ hours. Open the foil and fold it back to allow the turkey to get brown. Return to oven for about 30 minutes or until browned to your liking. Baste with pan drippings.

4. Remove to a heated serving platter; let rest about 20 minutes before carving. Garnish with parsley.

5. Put all the pan juices into a medium saucepan and boil down to half. This makes a delicious, easy sauce. Serve it in a sauce boat.

GIBLET STUFFING

Delicious way to use the turkey, or even chicken giblets that you may have in the house. Use all of the giblets, except the liver, which you can add to Chopped Liver, and the neck, which is not easy to handle.

    Turkey giblets
    4 matzot
    1 onion
    4 tbls. oil
    1 cup water
    2 eggs
    1 tsp. bouillon powder
    ½ tsp. salt
    Dash pepper

1. Chop the onion and fry it lightly in the oil. Cut the giblets into very small pieces and add them to the onion. Fry together for about 10 minutes. Add 1 cup water and cook for 20 minutes.

2. Break the *matzot* and put in a bowl. Add the fried onions, giblets and all the juices that have accumulated in the pan. Add the bouillon powder, salt, pepper and eggs. Mix well and stuff the bird.

SWEET AND SOUR CELERY

Refreshing and non-fattening; a brightly dressed spring vegetable addition to our menu.

    2 bunches celery hearts, stalks only
    2 cups water
    1½ tsp. salt
    ¼ cup lemon juice
    2 tbls. salad oil
    1/3 cup sugar
    ½ garlic clove, mashed
    1 tbls. potato starch

1. Clean the celery stalks and cut them diagonally in 1" pieces.

2. Bring the water and salt to a boil and add the celery. Bring to a boil again and cook for 10 minutes. The celery should be tender, yet hold its shape and retain some of its crispness. Add the sugar, lemon juice, salad oil and garlic. Cook for an additional 2 minutes.

3. Mix the potato starch with 2 tablespoons water. Add to the boiling celery. Mix well and cook for 2 minutes on reduced heat, until the liquid thickens slightly. Remove from heat. Serve hot or cold. You can reheat it if necessary.

FRUIT PIE—KOSHER LE'PESSACH
(Photograph on page 70)

The crust of this pie is crisp and delicate. The filling is quite simple to assemble, yet looks handsome and tastes good. Prepare ahead of time and avoid last minute rushing.

    Crust:
    1¼ cups matzo meal
    1 egg
    3 tbls. sugar
    4 oz. margarine (1 stick)

    Fruit filling:
    2 1-lb. cans peaches
    25 whole blanched almonds (1½ oz.)
    1 3-oz. pkg. gelatin, peach flavor

1. Preheat the oven to 400°F.

2. Cut the margarine into the *matzo meal* with a pastry blender until the pieces are the size of small peas. Add the sugar and salt. Beat the egg and blend in with fork. Form into a ball with your hands.

3. Flatten the ball in a greased pie pan, building up sides. Prick the bottom and sides with a fork. Bake in the hot oven for 12 to 15 minutes or until golden brown. Cool thoroughly.

4. Drain the fruit, reserving ½ cup of liquid. Dissolve gelatin in 1 cup of hot water and add the reserved ½ cup syrup. Cool until slightly thickened. Arrange the fruit nicely in the cool pie crust. Pour gelatin on top. Garnish with almonds, putting them on the slightly set gelatin in a symmetrical design.

Passover 'Filler-Uppers'

To comply with the strict dietary customs that forbid bread and leavened flour products, special foods are prepared during Passover. It takes some creativity and imagination to satisfy a family without bread, but Jewish mothers have found ways to prepare delicacies without violating the traditions. Through the generations, a pattern of Passover specialties have been formed and some of them are now favorites any time. One classic Passover 'original', the *matzo ball*, is identified with Jewish cookery as a whole, and is eaten all year round by Jews and non-Jews alike. *Matzo balls* are known also as *Kneidlach* and a recipe for them is given. (See index.)

In this section you will find recipes for many Passover specialties. All of them comply with the dietary laws and are outstanding too, as tasty, handsome dishes. Some are vintage recipes from olden days and others are creations of our own generation. These recipes are designed to avoid real or imaginary, hunger-pangs that the lack of bread may cause. Dishes like Passover 'Hot Rolls', 'Magic Dough', Noodles and *Blintzes* for Passover, *Bubaleh* (Pan-Cake), and Chocolate *Matzo Roll* will keep everybody happy as well as satisfied. All of the recipes rely on traditional stand-bys that substitute for flour during this holiday: *matzo meal,* potato starch, eggs, nuts, and of course, *matzot* themselves.

A 'Magic Dough' for Passover
Bagels
Cream Puffs
Soup Almonds
Passover 'Hot Rolls'
Noodles and Blintzes for Passover
Passover 'Pan-Cake'—Bubaleh
Chocolate Matzo Roll

A 'MAGIC DOUGH' FOR PASSOVER

How would you like to treat yourself to an absolutely *Kosher Le'Pesach Bagel?* You would love it, we know. And how about big golden cream puffs? We think you would love them too, filled with a variety of filling: chopped liver or sweet whipped cream, depending on when you serve them. You can have bagels and cream puffs by preparing the following recipe. It is a simple, basic dough made of eggs, *matzo meal*, water and fat. This dough is so versatile that you don't have to stop at bagels and cream puffs. Go on, and pre-

pare soup almonds, either baked or fried. Then you can also shape the dough into a big ring to make a round puffed cake, perfect for filling with whipped cream. From one batch of 'Magic Dough' you can have four bagels plus six cream puffs, plus two dozen baked soup almonds, plus one cup fried soup almonds. Enjoy, Enjoy.

For About 2 Cups of Dough

4 eggs
1 cup water
½ cup oil or 1 stick margarine
1 tsp. salt
1½ cups matzo meal

1. Bring the water, salt and fat to a quick boil in a medium saucepan. Remove from heat and add *matzo meal,* all at once. Stir well and return to heat for 3 minutes, stirring continuously. Remove from heat and let stand 10 minutes.

2. Add the eggs, one at a time, and mix vigorously to incorporate them in the dough. When all 4 eggs are mixed in, the dough is ready. You may start producing the goodies, according to preference.

BAGELS

For 8 Bagels
1 recipe 'Magic Dough'

1. Preheat the oven to 400°F.

2. Oil your hands and take 2 tablespoons of dough. Shape it into a little ball, then into a 5" 'rope'. Pinch the ends together to get a bagel shape.

3. Put on a greased cookie sheet.

4. Bake for about 40 minutes, or until nicely browned.

CREAM PUFFS

For 20 Cream Puffs
1 recipe 'Magic Dough'

1. Preheat the oven to 400°F.

2. Drop the dough by heaping tablespoons on a greased cookie sheet. Bake for 35 minutes, or until golden brown.

SOUP ALMONDS

1 recipe 'Magic Dough'

1. *To bake:* preheat oven to 400°F. Measure ½ teaspoon dough and shape in small balls between your hands. Put on a greased cookie sheet. Bake for about 15 minutes, until puffed and brown.

2. *To fry:* push the dough through a flat vegetable grater into a skillet of very hot oil. Fry until golden brown on both sides. Drain on paper.

PASSOVER 'HOT ROLLS'

Everyone looks forward to the special Passover delicacies, and to switching from bread to crisp *matzah.* The funny thing is that after a few days of eating *matzah* we crave something that will remind us of bread. Here you will find a recipe for Passover 'rolls'. They are nice to serve in the morning with coffee, for lunch and, of course, as a 'dinner roll' at a 'dairy' dinner. The 'rolls' are based on the idea of popovers, and you will need a muffin tin to make them.

For 10 to 12 'Rolls'
3 eggs
1 cup milk
2/3 cup matzo meal
4 tbls. potato starch
½ tsp. salt
Dash pepper
2 tbls. oil

1. Preheat the oven to 475°F, and grease muffin tins.

2. Mix the eggs, milk, *matzo meal,* potato starch, salt and pepper in a large bowl. Beat the mixture well for about 2 minutes with an electric or hand beater.

3. Add the oil and continue beating for 1 minute.

4. Pour the mixture in the well-greased muffin tins, filling each cup only ¾ full.

5. Bake in the hot oven for 15 minutes, then lower the heat to 350°F and bake for another 30 minutes. Serve hot.

NOODLES AND BLINTZES FOR PASSOVER

I still remember my surprise, as a child, at seeing noodles in my chicken soup at a Passover meal. Mother assured me that her noodles were okay because they were made of eggs. She also taught me the secrets of preparing Passover *blintzes* from the same 'dough'. And to tell you the truth, those noodles and *blintzes* for Passover tasted better on the holiday than the regular ones, all year round.

For 12 Blintzes, or 6 Servings of Noodles
3 eggs
11/3 cups water
6 tbls. potato starch
½ tsp. salt
Dash pepper (only for noodles)
3 tsp. oil
Oil for the skillet

1. In a medium bowl mix the eggs, potato starch, water, salt and oil very thoroughly. The mixture should look like thick cream.

2. Heat a heavy 5″ skillet. Sprinkle with a few drops of oil and grease the whole skillet with a paper towel. Continue heating until a drop of water will dance on the skillet.

3. Put 2 tablespoons of batter into the skillet. Tilt to spread the batter evenly on the surface. When the batter in the skillet looks completely dry, turn over and fry on the other side. Regulate the heat and the frying time so that each pancake will be pale gold.

4. Invert the skillet above a plate. The pancake will fall on the plate. Continue making thin pancakes until you finish the batter.

5. To make noodles, let the pancakes cool. Roll up, and cut crosswise, to 1/8″ width noodles. Use in soups.

6. To make *blintzes*, fill the pancakes with your favorite Passover cheese filling. Roll up and heat in a skillet before serving.

PASSOVER 'PAN CAKE'—BUBALEH

Here is a quick Passover 'Pan Cake' that you may serve with wine or liqueur to guests who drop in unexpectedly during the holiday. Cut it into cubes and sprinkle sugar on top. We call it *Bubaleh* at home.

For 4 Servings

2 eggs, separated
1/4 cup matzo meal
2 tbls. potato starch
1/2 tsp. salt
2 tbls. sugar
Oil for frying
1 tsp. lemon rind, grated

1. Whip the egg whites with the salt until foamy. Gradually add the sugar. The whipped egg whites should look firm and glossy but not dry. Beat the yolks and add gently to the whites.

2. Sprinkle the *matzo meal* and potato starch over the egg mixture and fold in gently. Add the grated lemon rind. The volume of the eggs should not diminish. Use a big spoon or spatula for the folding.

3. Put some oil in a 9″ skillet and grease the whole surface. Heat the skillet thoroughly then pour in the 'pan cake' mixture. Brown on one side, then turn with a big spatula and brown on the other side.

4. Turn on to a plate, cut in cubes or quarters, sprinkle with sugar and serve warm. You may also sprinkle sweet wine or sweet liqueur on the *Bubaleh.*

CHOCOLATE MATZO ROLL
(Photograph on page 70)

An Israeli version of a non-bake Passover cake. The chocolate *matzo roll* has to be chilled before it can be sliced to reveal the enjoyable combination of smoothness and crunchiness. The roll is covered with a shiny chocolate glaze.

4 Matzot unsalted
8 oz. margarine (2 sticks)
6 oz. semi-sweet chocolate
3 tbls. strong black coffee
1/4 cup sugar
1 tbls. brandy
3 oz. chopped walnuts

1. Moisten the *matzot* under running water, then crumble into a medium bowl.

2. Melt the sugar, coffee and 4 ounces of the chocolate in the top of a double boiler. Remove from heat when thoroughly combined, add the brandy and cool slightly.

3. Beat the margarine until fluffy and add the melted chocolate gradually, beating well after each addition. Stir in the crumbled *matzot* and chopped nuts; mix with a tablespoon.

4. Pour the mixture lengthwise on a piece of waxed paper 12″ long. Fold paper around mixture and shape like a salami. Roll on table under your palms to give a smooth, round appearance. Secure edges of paper. Refrigerate roll for 6 hours.

5. When hard enough to cut peel off the paper, prepare the chocolate glaze and pour on top of the roll. Chill again. Serve the roll cold, sliced crosswise.

6. To prepare the glaze, melt the remaining chocolate with 3 tablespoons water in top of a double boiler.

Whipped Desserts and Cakes

(Photograph on page 84)

Special attention is given to the sweet things in life in the following pages. We found, from our own experience, that sweets and desserts, particularly cakes, are the items most-missed during Passover. It may be a psychological reaction to the prohibition of bread or just another way of manifesting a gala holiday mood. Whatever the reason, we offer here many recipes for luscious cakes and mouth-watering desserts. You are invited to enjoy them as the last course of a meal or as refreshments when guests come to say 'Happy Passover.'

The variety of basic ingredients for these desserts and cakes includes eggs, fruits, chocolate, whipped cream, almonds, nuts and much more. The results are wonderful, too. We are sure that after their formal introduction as Passover treats they will visit your kitchen any time of the year.

Passover High-Rise Torte
Chocolate Icing
A Thing of Beauty
Strawberry Syrup
Chocolate Crown
Chocolate Filling
Meringue Shells
Coconut Macaroons
Passover Sponge Cake
Chocolate Mousse

PASSOVER HIGH-RISE TORTE
(Photograph on page 84)

The nut torte is an integral part of Passover's delicious *repertoire*. When properly prepared this cake rises high and is very handsome indeed. Chocolate icing gives it a delectable final touch.

7 large eggs at room temperature
2/3 cup potato starch
2/3 cup matzo meal
1 cup ground nuts
2 tbls. salad oil
1 1/3 cup sugar
Juice of a whole lemon
1 tsp. grated lemon rind

1. Remove the eggs from the refrigerator 1 hour before starting the cake. Set out a large tube pan, 10″ x 4¼″; do not oil it, just have it handy. Preheat the oven to 375°F.

2. Separate the eggs. Put the whites in a big bowl and the yolks in a medium one.

3. Sift the *matzo meal* twice to a very fine consistency. Measure ⅔ cup. Then sift together with the potato starch. Grind the nuts to a very fine grain and measure 1 cup.

4. Beat the yolks and gradually add half of the sugar. Add the oil and 2 tablespoons water. The mixture should be thick and bright. Add the lemon juice and lemon rind.

5. Beat the egg whites until foamy, then, still beating gradually add the remaining sugar. Beat until the whites look stiff and glossy and hold their shape. Do not overbeat.

6. Add 1 tablespoon beaten egg white to the yolk mixture to make it fluffy. Fold the yolks into the whites very gently with a big spatula.

7. Gently fold in the *matzo meal* and potato starch a little at a time. Finally fold in the ground nuts.

8. Pour the batter in the tube pan. Reduce the heat in the oven to 350°F. Put the pan in the middle lower third of the oven and bake for 60 to 70 minutes. Insert a toothpick. If it comes out dry, the cake is ready.

9. Cool the cake in the pan 1 hour.

Chocolate Icing
3 oz. semi-sweet chocolate
6 tbls. water
1 tbls. brandy
1/3 cup sugar
3 tbls. margarine
16 walnut halves (1 oz.)

1. Heat the water on a low flame. Break the chocolate into small pieces and add to the warm water. The chocolate should melt gently and slowly so it will not scorch or get dry.

2. Add the brandy, sugar, and margarine to the melted chocolate. Cook for about 4 minutes, until the mixture gets thick and even.

3. Pour the icing while still hot on top of the cake. Let it 'drip' down the sides.

4. Arrange the walnut halves in a circle on top of the cake. When you serve, cut between the nuts so that each slice will have its own walnut.

A THING OF BEAUTY
(Photograph on page 84)

This beautiful meringue layer cake is a real treasure for Passover. It is light, airy, and delicate. When filled with fresh strawberries and whipped cream, then garnished with peaches and mint leaves, it is truly a thing of beauty. Follow the instructions carefully for whipping and baking the meringue layers and the cake will come out exactly as in the picture.

Meringue layers:
3 egg whites at room temperature
1 cup sugar
1 tsp. lemon juice

Fillings and garnishes:
1½ baskets strawberries
1 cup whipping cream
4 halves of canned peaches
Mint leaves

1. Preheat the oven to 275°F (slow oven). Line 2 cookie sheets with waxed paper. Draw a 9″ circle on each. You can use a large plate as your guide and trace around it with a pencil. Grease the paper lightly with salad oil.

2. Put the egg whites in a large bowl. Start whipping until big bubbles begin to form. Add 2 tablespoons sugar and whip until dissolved. This takes at least 2 minutes. Continue adding 2 tablespoons sugar and beating 2 minutes after each addition. When all sugar is dissolved, whip for a full 10 minutes more at high speed, adding the lemon juice gradually. The meringue should be stiff and shiny.

3. Divide the meringue in two parts. Put each in the center of a drawn circle on each cookie sheet. With a big spoon or spatula spread the meringue to form a perfect round, using the tracing as a guide. Smooth tops with a spatula. (You can pipe the meringue through a large pastry bag with a big star tip to make a fancy design, like the one in the picture, if you wish.)

4. Lower oven temperature to 250°F. Put the meringue in oven, one above the other or side by side. Be sure there is room for the heat to circulate freely around them. Bake for 1 hour, turn off heat, set door ajar and dry meringue for 1 hour.

5. Remove from the oven and cool slightly on a rack. Peel the paper off gently. Prepare the filling and topping while the meringue cools.

6. Clean and hull the strawberries. Save half a basket for preparing a syrup; leave the rest whole or slice lengthwise.

7. Whip the cream and sweeten to taste. Put a meringue on a flat serving platter. Spread with half the whipped cream and cover with half the sliced strawberries. Put the other meringue on top and spread with the remaining whipped cream. Put the peach halves in the center. Arrange some sliced and some whole strawberries in a nice design around the peaches.

8. Refrigerate. Just before serving drizzle with strawberry syrup and garnish with mint leaves.

Strawberry Syrup
½ basket strawberries
¾ cup sugar
½ cup water

1. Cook the water and sugar on medium-high heat for 10 minutes or until a drop forms a small ball in a cup of cold water.

2. Mash the strawberries lightly and add to the syrup. Cook for 3 to 5 minutes, stirring constantly. If the syrup looks too hard, add 2 tablespoons water. Cool slightly and drizzle over strawberries on top of cake.

3. If you prepare the syrup ahead of time, you will have to re-heat on a very low flame to make it syrupy again. Cool to room temperature and use.

CHOCOLATE CROWN
(Photograph on page 84)

This handsome meringue crown has a delicate color of white with some shades of ivory. The meringue is pleasantly crisp, and when filled with a creamy chocolate filling causes instant compliments. A large pastry bag is needed for shaping the crown. Follow the directions carefully and your crown will be as nice as the one in the picture.

Meringue crown:
3 egg whites at room temperature
1 cup sugar
1 tsp. lemon juice

1. Preheat the oven to 275°F. Line a cookie sheet with waxed paper and draw an 8″ circle on it. Grease the paper lightly with salad oil.

2. Put the egg whites in a large bowl and start whipping. When light foam forms add 2 tablespoons sugar. Whip until the sugar dissolves. Add 2 more tablespoons sugar and whip again. Repeat until you use all the sugar. The time for dissolving each addition of sugar is about 2 minutes. When all the sugar is incorporated whip, at a high speed, 10 full minutes more, adding the lemon juice gradually.

3. To duplicate the crown in the picture you will need a clean pastry bag fitted with a large decorating nozzle. Fill the bag with whipped whites and press out on the lined cookie sheet, using the drawing as your guide.

4. As you can see, the crown is comprised of 3 layers: a base layer, which serves as the bottom of the crown and two more layers, built one upon the other, to form the walls.

5. To make the base layer pipe out small, equal rosettes around the circle on the waxed paper. The rosettes should touch each other to form a complete border. Fill the inside of this border with whipped whites, using a spoon or spatula to spread them over the entire bottom. You should have a flat, even layer about ¾″ thick.

6. The second layer is made of two rows of piped-out rosettes: one visible from the outside, and the other invisible, built inside for more support. Pipe the first row directly over the border of the base layer. The inner row about ½″ away from the outer one.

7. The third, and last, layer is piped on top of the second one, supported by the two rows.

8. Reduce the oven temperature to 250°F. Put the crown shell in, and bake for 1 hour, without opening the door. Turn off heat, set door ajar and let the crown dry in the oven for 1 hour more.

9. Remove the crown from the oven and chill. Peel the paper carefully because cake is very brittle. You may choose not to peel the paper, and only trim the edges around the crown with scissors.

10. When the crown is completely chilled, fill with chocolate filling, cover and refrigerate until serving time.

Chocolate Filling
1 cup whipping cream
6 oz. semi-sweet chocolate
1 tsp. instant coffee
1 tbls. brandy
Chocolate shavings

1. Whip the cream until it stands in soft peaks and holds its shape. Do not over beat.

2. Put the chocolate in top of a double boiler, over simmering water and melt gently. Add 3

All of the desserts in this picture are based on whipped eggs. They are delicious, good looking and of course Kosher Le'Pessach. The name we gave the meringue layer cake at the top of the picture is A THING OF BEAUTY (recipe on page 82), and it is beautiful indeed. The dessert in the middle is a CHOCOLATE CROWN (recipe on page 83), crisp and airy on the outside, filled with rich, smooth chocolate-flavored whipped cream inside. At bottom is the PASSOVER HIGH-RISE TORTE (recipe on page 81). The preparation of this cake includes an unusual stretching technique that produces surprising results.

tablespoons hot water and the instant coffee. Stir until chocolate is smooth and satiny. Remove from heat. Add the brandy and cool slightly, for about 3 to 5 minutes.

3. Fold chocolate into the whipped cream gently. (You may also beat the chocolate into the whipped cream at a very slow speed.) Chill in the refrigerator for about 10 minutes. It is now ready to go in the crown.

4. Use the same pastry decorating bag you used for the crown. Press the whipped chocolate filling inside the crown to make rosettes. The filling should be a little higher than the crown walls.

5. To make chocolate shavings use a vegetable peeler that is slightly heated. Shave the side of a chocolate bar directly on top of the crown.

MERINGUE SHELLS
(Photograph on page 70)

Crisp, delicate shells to hold a variety of delicious fillings, their ivory color makes a beautiful frame for white whipped cream, red strawberries and green mint leaves, as shown in the picture. Try them, too, with rich Chocolate Filling (see above).

For 6 Shells

3 egg whites at room temperature
1 cup fine sugar
Dash salt
1 tsp. lemon juice

1. Preheat the oven to 250°F. Remove the eggs from the refrigerator about an hour before starting.

2. Whip the egg whites with the salt. When they become foamy very gradually add the sugar, 2 tablespoons at a time. Whip after each addition until there are no traces of sugar. After all the sugar is mixed in, continue whipping at high speed for 10 minutes. The meringue should be stiff and glossy.

3. Line a greased cookie sheeet with waxed paper. Draw 6 circles, 3″ in diameter on the paper with a pencil. You can use a small round plate for this. Lightly grease the paper with salad oil.

4. Spread each circle with some meringue and use a pastry bag with a ½″ tip to pipe out and build the edges around the base.

5. Bake for 1 hour. Turn off the heat, set door

ajar and let the meringue shells dry for 1 hour.

6. Peel off the waxed paper very carefully. Fill with the filling of your choice.

COCONUT MACAROONS

Light and airy, the macaroons are a traditional Passover specialty made of whipped egg whites, spiked with crunchy shredded coconut.

For 30 Macaroons

3 egg whites at room temperature
8 oz. coconut flakes (2½ cups)
1 cup fine sugar
1 tbls. lemon juice

1. Take the eggs out of the refrigerator 1 hour before starting the macaroons.

2. Preheat the oven to 300°F. Lightly grease a cookie sheet with salad oil. Line it with waxed paper and grease the paper, too.

3. Whip the whites until they start to hold their shape. Add the sugar, 2 tablespoons at a time, and whip 2 minutes after each addition. When all the sugar is dissolved, whip another 5 minutes, adding the lemon juice gradually.

4. Sprinkle the coconut a little at a time on the top of the meringue and fold in gently. Repeat until all the coconut is mixed with the meringue.

5. Form little mounds of batter on the cookie sheet with a spoon or pastry bag. Bake for 20 minutes until the macaroons are ivory in color. Turn off the oven, set door ajar and leave macaroons for another 20 minutes.

6. Cool on a rack. Separate from the paper by carefully peeling it off the bottom of the cookies.

PASSOVER SPONGE CAKE

This cake is a small wonder. It is tall and light with a beautiful color, yet there is not a speck of flour in it.

6 eggs at room temperature
½ cup matzo meal
4 tbls. potato starch
½ tsp. salt
1 cup sugar
1 lemon, for juice and rind
1 tbls. salad oil

1. Preheat the oven to 350°F. Lightly grease a 9″ round pan.

2. Sift and measure the *matzo meal* and the potato starch. Sift together.

3. Separate the eggs. Put the whites in a large bowl, and yolks in a medium one. Beat the yolks with the oil and 1 tablespoon of lemon juice until thick and lemon-colored.

4. Whip the whites with the salt. When the peaks start to form add the sugar, 1 tablespoon at a time, beating well after each addition. The whipped egg whites should be stiff, but not too dry.

5. Add egg yolk mixture to the meringue, folding in very gently with a big spoon or spatula.

6. Fold in the dry ingredients a little at a time. Fold gently after each addition. It is a good idea to add the dry ingredients through a sieve rather than directly from a measuring cup. This assures even distribution.

7. Grate the lemon peel on a fine grater. Fold into the batter.

8. Pour the batter gently into the pan. Spread evenly without pressing. Bake for about 40 minutes or until a toothpick comes out dry and clean. Cool and remove from pan.

CHOCOLATE MOUSSE
(Photograph on page 70)

A classic creation of the gourmet kitchen comes to you here in a new *Kosher Le'Pessach* version. Please note that the cooling time is at least six hours, so plan accordingly.

For 8 to 10 Servings

4 eggs
1 tsp. potato starch
1/3 cup sugar
1 cup milk
1½ tbls. unflavored gelatin
1/3 cup strong black coffee
6 oz. semi-sweet chocolate
1 tbls. brandy
1 cup whipping cream

1. Separate the eggs. Put the yolks in the top part of a double boiler away from the heat. Put the whites in a large mixing bowl. Soften the gelatin in 1/3 cup water.

2. Beat the yolks and add the sugar gradually. When thick and lemon-colored, add the potato starch and milk in a slow stream, beating continually. Add the softened gelatin.

3. Heat water in the bottom part of the double boiler. Put the top pot, with the yolk mixture, over bottom. Do not let water touch top. Simmer gently until gelatin dissolves and the mixture coats a metal spoon, for about 5 to 7 minutes. Remove from heat and add brandy.

4. Combine chocolate and coffee in a medium saucepan and put on top of double boiler or over very low heat. Do not let chocolate scorch. (An equivalent amount of water, mixed with 1 heaping teaspoon of instant coffee may be substituted for the coffee called for.) Add melted chocolate to yolk mixture, stir and cool about an hour. Do not refrigerate.

5. When cool and almost set, whip egg whites until they form soft peaks and hold their shape. Fold gently into chocolate mixture.

6. Whip cream until it stands in soft peaks and fold half into chocolate mixture. Blend well and pour in a 4-cup mold. Cover with waxed paper and refrigerate at least 6 hours, or overnight. Refrigerate remaining whipped cream, covered, for garnishing later.

7. Unmold the mousse on a plate about an hour before serving. Garnish with reserved whipped cream and chill until needed.

To Unmold: run a knife along the edges of the mold, then dip mold in hot water for 10 seconds. Invert on a serving plate and shake gently. If the mousse does not slide out readily, dip briefly in hot water once more.

Passover Nutty Specialties

Nuts have special significance on Passover which is why we use them so many ways: *Haroset,* one of the *Seder's* symbolic foods and in many gourmet dishes as well. Their meat is rich, delicate, moist yet crunchy, so they lend themselves to a number of varied treatments from pre-dinner cocktails to after-dinner fruit and cheese. They give new dimension to ordinary dishes, too.

But nuts at Passover are not merely for eating. The youngsters stuff the pockets of their newly-purchased clothes with nuts of all kinds and use them as the basis for all sorts of traditional holiday games.

Stuffed Mushrooms
Walnut 'Sandwiches'
Cheese-Nut Ball
A Very Special Nut Roulade
Filbert Cookies
Nut Bonbons
Almond-Chocolate Macaroons

STUFFED MUSHROOMS
(Photograph on page 88)

A different but delicious appetizer or companion for cocktails. The mushrooms are sautéed in butter and white wine, then stuffed with spiced sour cream and garnished with a nut.

For 24 Stuffed Mushrooms

24 white mushrooms (1 lb.)
3 tbls. butter
1/3 cup dry white wine

Sour cream filling:

1 cup sour cream
1 tbls. lemon juice
1 tsp. salt
Dash of pepper
24 pecan halves (1½ oz.)

1. Clean mushrooms and cut out stems.

2. Melt the butter and sauté the mushrooms in it. Add the wine, cover the pan and cook, on low heat, for several minutes. Remove from heat and arrange the caps, open side upwards, on a jelly roll pan or other baking sheet.

3. Cut the stems in small bits and sauté in the pan juices.

4. Mix the sour cream with lemon juice, salt, pepper and bits of sautéed stems. Fill the caps with this mixture and put a nut on top. Can be prepared in advance to this point.

5. Just before serving, bake in a 450°F oven for 5 minutes. Serve hot.

WALNUT 'SANDWICHES'
(Photograph on page 88)

Miniature nut 'sandwiches', stuffed with cheese, are delicious when served as an appetizer or party snack.

For About 25 'Sandwiches'

4 oz. walnut halves
3 oz. cream cheese at room temperature
1 tsp. salt
Dash pepper
Parsley

1. Beat the cheese with salt and pepper until smooth.

2. Put 1 teaspoon of the cheese on a walnut half. Cover with another half and press together lightly. Arrange on a tray and garnish with parsley.

The sign, suspended at the back says, in Hebrew, Hag Sameach (Happy Holiday). All the goodies here are based on nuts. In the glass container are FILBERT COOKIES (recipe on page 90). Next is the VERY SPECIAL NUT ROULADE (recipe on page 89), one of the lightest and most delicate cakes you have ever tasted. Farther down is the piquant CHEESE-NUT BALL (recipe on page 89) with sliced apples that go so well with it. At the bottom, left, is a plate with STUFFED MUSHROOMS (recipe on page 87), and WALNUT SANDWICHES (recipe on page 87) on a bed of parsley. To the right, in another glass container, are ALMOND CHOCOLATE MACAROONS (recipe on page 90), which melt in your mouth when eaten.

CHEESE-NUT BALL
(Photograph on page 88)

Handy to have around, especially if you are expecting company, this cheese ball can be prepared several days in advance. Its taste even improves under refrigeration. The ball is covered with chopped walnuts and is lovely to look at. Arrange pieces of thin *matzah* and slices of fresh fruit around the ball. The pleasure is all yours.

12 oz. cream cheese
4 oz. very sharp Cheddar-type cheese
1 small onion
½ bell pepper
1 tbls. snipped parsley
2 tbls. brandy
1 tsp. salt
¼ tsp. white pepper
½ cup chopped walnuts

1. Bring the cream cheese to room temperature. Grate the Cheddar on a very fine grater. Peel the onion and chop very finely. Chop the bell pepper into small cubes.

2. Combine the cheese with the onion, pepper and parsley. Add salt, white pepper, brandy and mix well. Chill in the refrigerator until it hardens enough to handle conveniently.

3. Form a ball of cheese and roll in the chopped walnuts. Cover completely. Wrap in a piece of aluminum foil; chill for 6 hours or overnight.

A VERY SPECIAL NUT ROULADE
(Photograph on page 88)

A real treat all year around, this cake will be especially appreciated on Passover since it does not have any flour in it. The delicious substitute for flour is ground filberts. The roulade is filled with sweet whipped cream then topped with chocolate shavings and candied cherries.

Dough:
4 eggs at room temperature
¾ cup fine sugar
Dash salt
½ cup finely ground filberts
¼ cup matzo meal, sifted
1 tbls. potato starch

Whipped cream filling:
1 cup whipping cream
¼ cup fine sugar
1 tbls. brandy

Garnish:
1 oz. semi-sweet chocolate bar
12 cherries
12 whole filberts or other nuts

1. Eggs at room temperature behave much better so, about an hour before beginning preparations, take eggs from refrigerator.

2. Preheat the oven to 375° just before you start. Grease a jelly roll pan lightly and line with waxed paper and grease paper lightly, also.

3. Separate the eggs. Put yolks in one large mixing bowl, and whites in another. Beat yolks with an electric or rotary beater, and add sugar very gradually. Beat after each addition until sugar dissolves and yolks are thick and very pale.

4. While beating at a lower speed, add ground filberts, *matzo meal*, potato starch, and a dash salt. The mixture should be very smooth.

5. Clean and dry the beaters. Whip egg whites until they hold their shape and cling to beaters. Do not overbeat.

6. The success of this cake depends on the way the yolk-filbert mixture is combined with the whipped egg whites. Transfer about one-fourth of the whites to the yolk-filbert mixture and fold in very gently. This will lighten the mixture and enable it to absorb more readily another quarter of the egg whites. Continue adding and folding whites until all are combined with the yolk-filbert mixture. The result is a light, fluffy batter.

7. Pour the batter into prepared pan. Bake for 15 to 20 minutes until an inserted toothpick comes out dry.

8. Spread a clean kitchen towel on the counter and dust lightly with sugar. Turn cake over the towel and remove from the pan. Peel paper off very gently and roll the cake lengthwise, with towel over it, jelly roll fashion. Let cool.

9. When cake is completely cool, prepare filling: Whip the cream, adding sugar and brandy at the last stages of whipping.

10. Open the rolled cake and quickly spread with half of the whipped cream. Roll back. Spread the other half on the top and sides of the roulade.

11. Garnish top of cake with chocolate shavings, whole nuts and candied cherries.

FILBERT COOKIES
(Photograph on page 88)

Crisp cookies made of *matzo meal* and almonds with filberts hidden in their center. The cookies will become such favorites that you had better prepare lots of them.

For 30 Cookies
¾ cup matzo meal
1½ cups pulverized almonds (6 ozs.)
4 oz. margarine
1 egg
½ cup sugar
1 tbls. brandy
30 filberts

1. Preheat the oven to 400°F. Line a cookie sheet with waxed paper.

2. Mix dry ingredients, except filberts.

3. Cut in the margarine with pastry blender or fork until pieces are the size of small peas.

4. Add the egg and brandy. Blend well. (It is best to do the final blending with fingertips.)

5. Moisten hands, make small balls of dough 1″ in diameter. Shape each ball around a filbert.

6. Arrange 1″ apart on cookie sheet. Bake for 12 to 15 minutes, until golden brown.

7. Cool cookies thoroughly. Sprinkle with sugar.

NUT BONBONS
(Photograph on page 70)

Tasty, tiny 'finger food' dessert made of walnuts filled with a delicate filling, dipped in chocolate and topped with pistachio nuts. These little morsels will be more than welcome at the end of a meal or with a cup of coffee.

For 20 Bonbons
40 walnut halves (3 oz.)
20 tiny paper cups
½ cup fine sugar
3 tbls. margarine
1 tbls. brandy
3 oz. semi-sweet chocolate
20 peeled pistachio nuts

1. Select nice looking unbroken walnuts. Plunge them in hot water and rinse under running water. Drain on paper towels then dry on a cookie sheet in a 250°F oven for 15 minutes. Cool completely.

2. Put the sugar in a clean, dry blender. Blend on high speed for 3 minutes until pulverized. Beat the margarine in a medium bowl with sugar and brandy until the sugar dissolves completely.

3. Spread a little sugar filling on 20 walnut halves; top with the remaining halves. Press lightly to hold together. When all 'sandwiches' are ready chill for 1 hour in the refrigerator.

4. Melt the chocolate with 2 tablespoons water in top of a double boiler over low heat. Dip half of each 'sandwich' in the melted chocolate. Put in a paper cup. When all are ready press a pistachio nut on each.

ALMOND CHOCOLATE MACAROONS
(Photograph on page 88)

Almonds give these light, delicate cookies a tender crunchiness and special quality. The secret of their success is in patiently whipping the egg whites, then mixing them gently with the chocolate.

For 30 Macaroons
6 oz. semi-sweet chocolate
3 egg whites at room temperature
½ cup sugar
Dash salt
¾ cup almonds, slivered

1. Preheat the oven to 350°F. Grease a cookie sheet lightly with salad oil, line with waxed paper and grease the paper, too.

2. Break up the chocolate and put in the top of a double boiler. Place over hot water and let melt very gently.

3. Whip the egg whites with a dash of salt until they stand in soft peaks. Add the sugar, 1 tablespoon at a time, whipping continuously after each addition until the sugar dissolves completely. Continue whipping until you get a stiff, glossy meringue. At least 5 minutes.

4. Remove melted chocolate from boiler. Add about one-fourth of the meringue to melted chocolate and fold in gently. Add another one-fourth and fold again. Now, add the fluffed chocolate to the remaining meringue, and fold gently.

5. Fold the almonds in gently. Drop the chocolate meringue onto the greased cookie sheet from a teaspoon. Bake for about 10 minutes, and remove immediately from oven. Cool on a rack and peel the waxed paper gently off the cookies.

VIII

YOM HA'ATZMAUT:
ISRAEL'S REBIRTH CREATES
A NEW CUISINE

YOM HA'ATZMAUT, Israel's Independence Day, comes on the Fifth of the Hebrew month of Iyar. The establishment of the Jewish State, in May 1948, was the realization of a two-thousand year hope to return to the Land of Israel and live there as a free people. During twenty centuries of living in the diaspora, the Jews maintained close emotional ties with the homeland from which they were expelled by the Roman Legions. While wandering all over the world they yearned for their own land, expressing their longings through daily prayers and holiday celebrations. After Israel achieved statehood Jews from more than seventy countries settled in Israel to take part in the unique experience of rebuilding their own country.

Yom Ha'Atzmaut is celebrated throughout Israel with throngs of people parading in the streets dancing, singing and generally having a good time. Stages are set up in the city squares where theatrical groups and singers entertain the crowds. Israeli flags fly high, as do fireworks, and everybody re-lives the excitement of the Declaration of Independence. Foreign diplomats extend their governments' greetings to the President of Israel, while in Israeli Embassies around the world receptions are held for well-wishers.

Israel is a young state and as yet there are no traditional foods exclusively for *Yom Ha'Atzmaut*. On the other hand, a new and typical everyday cuisine is emerging. As a melting pot of cultures, habits and food preferences of immigrants from many countries, Israel's cooking is multi-flavored and multi-colored; Jews from Europe brought spicy Hungarian dishes, heavy German style meals, delicate Viennese pastry, even some specialties in the best French tradition. Those from Mediterranean regions brought the foods of their 'old countries': Greek appetizers, Turkish Sweets, and Middle Eastern dishes such as *Hummus, Tahinah, Pitah* and *Falafel*. All are adopted and adapted to the Israeli kitchen.

The emerging Israeli cuisine is unusual, marked as it is by the integration of many different kitchens; by the pride Israelis find in their creative cookery and by the joy they take in the reciprocity of eating traditions. Each ethnic group contributes something of its own and adopts much from the others, making the cuisine diversified and interesting. Israel's natural resources, too, have influenced the national menu. A scarcity of meat and an abundance of fresh fruit and vegetables, fish and poultry, account for many healthy, vitamin-rich dishes ranging from appetizers to desserts. The Israeli way of life, which embraces informality, directed the style of cooking, serving, and eating.

[91]

A colorful Israeli batik is the background for the JAFFA CHICKEN (recipe on page 97). The small salt and pepper shakers are Israeli, too.

Formal affairs are very rare: festive meals and entertaining are done family-style, which puts everybody at ease, including the hostess.

An Israeli menu features many salads of cooked and raw vegetables. A simple one that is widely enjoyed consists of every seasonal vegetable one can lay his hands on, chopped and seasoned with lemon juice, olive oil, salt and pepper. A whole family of dishes is built around eggplant: from piquant Middle Eastern salads to Vegetarian 'Chopped Liver,' depending on the origin of the cook. Fish is another favored food with preparations running the gamut from European Jewish traditional *gefilte fish* to Eastern fish in peppery tomato sauce. Poultry is prepared in new and imaginative ways, bringing together exotic spices from one ethnic group, cooking methods from another, with indigenous Israeli ingredients such as oranges, olives and grapes. All of these different dishes are combined on a typical, national menu and are enjoyed by all. When watching an Israeli of European extraction relishing a dish of Middle Eastern origin one appreciates fully the meaning of integration.

An Israeli-Style Get-Together

Entertaining Israeli-style can be most enjoyable. By adopting the Israeli spirit of friendliness and informality you and your guests can have a ball. The best way to handle such a relaxed affair is to use your dining table as a buffet, where all the dishes are ready to be savored. Your guests, in casual attire, can serve themselves from a variety of foods, sampling all and coming back for seconds as they wish.

An Israeli-style gathering can be held in the late afternoon, evening, or night: whatever the hour the dishes will be basically the same. They are favorite Israeli dishes, diversified in taste, texture and origin—as diversified as the people of Israel themselves.

Our menu is designed for a dinner get-together and is, therefore, somewhat elaborate. At any other Israeli-style gathering you can pick and choose just a few dishes from this menu. We start with a variety of cold brightly-flavored salads and dips, composed mainly of cooked vegetables that can be prepared ahead. A beautiful fish mold, Israeli Sea Delicacy, can double as the centerpiece for a cold buffet. For those who like it hot there is *Falafel*, little fried balls that are stuffed into *Pitah*, a thin round bread. *Falafel* is eaten with an Israeli Vegetable Salad, topped with *Tahinah* Dip (for recipe see index). The hot *Falafel* and the fresh salad are the only two courses that have to be prepared at the last minute. Despite the extra work the combination will be the highlight of this affair. It will rate especially high with teenagers. As a main course we have Jaffa Chicken, served with steamed rice and Zucchini in Tomato Sauce. The dessert is a colorful Fresh Fruit Dessert.

MENU
(planned for 8 to 12)
Israeli Sea Delicacy*
Hummus,* An Israeli Favorite
Tahinah—Eggplant Salad*
Vegetarian 'Chicken Liver'*
Pitah, Middle Eastern Bread*
Falafel*
Israeli Vegetable Salad*
Jaffa Chicken*
Zucchini in Tomato Sauce*
Pickles
Olives
Fresh Fruit Dessert*
Recipe given

ISRAELI SEA DELICACY

For Israelis, Fish Filet has a very special meaning. It brings back memories of the early days of the state when the economic situation was low, but spirits were high, as always. Fish filets were on the Israeli table day in and day out, so housewives tried to make them more interesting and tasty: from frozen fish they came up with goulash, schnitzel, croquettes, and even a type of *gefilte fish*.

In our recipe, the filets are molded with *tahinah* and pine nuts to create an impressive center dish, with an unmistakeable Israeli flavor.

1 lb. fish filets (fresh or frozen)
1½ cups water
½ cup white wine
1 onion, sliced
3 carrots
1 celery stalk, cut up
1 tsp. salt
⅛ tsp. pepper
2 tbls. unflavored gelatin
1 cup Tahina Dip (see index)
1/3 cup pine nuts

For garnish:
Tomato slices
Cucumber slices
Lemon slices
Black olives
Pimiento
Shredded lettuce

1. Thaw the filets.

2. Combine the water, wine and vegetables in a large shallow saucepan. Add salt and pepper; cook, covered for 10 minutes.

3. Add the filets and simmer gently for 20 minutes. Remove fish to a bowl. Strain the stock and measure 2 cups. If needed, add more white wine to make the full amount. Reserve the carrots for garnish.

4. Soften the gelatin in ⅓ cup water. Combine with the clear stock and boil 2 to 3 minutes until gelatin dissolves completely. Let cool, until almost set.

5. Flake the fish in small pieces with a fork. Add the cooled gelatin-stock, *Tahinah* Dip and pine nuts. Pour into a big fish-shaped mold.

6. Cover the mold with waxed paper and chill for at least 6 hours.

7. To unmold, run a knife around the edges, dip mold in hot water for 10 seconds and invert on a big serving plate.

8. To garnish, slice the carrots to make half-circle scales and long strips for fins and tail. Following the picture, stick 'scales' and 'fins' on the fish right after unmolding. Decorate the serving plate with the garnishing ingredients.

HUMMUS, AN ISRAELI FAVORITE

Hummus, made mainly of garbanzo beans (chick peas), has the consistency of a dip. A piquant appetizer, introduced to the nation by Middle Easterners, it is now enjoyed by all Israelis regardless of the place of origin and is a splendid example of the integration that has occurred in the national cuisine.

For 3½ Cups

½ lb. dried garbanzo beans (1 cup)
3 tbls. lemon juice
2 garlic cloves, mashed
3 tsp. salt
⅛ tsp. pepper
½ cup Tahinah Dip (see index)
3 tbls. olive oil

For garnish:
Olive oil
Parsley, snipped
Sweet paprika
Olives
Pickles

1. Cover the beans with water and soak overnight in large pot. They will soften slightly and double in volume.

2. Drain the beans, rinse and cover again with water; add 2 teaspoons of salt. Cover pot, bring to a boil, reduce heat and simmer for about 1½ hours, or until tender.

3. Drain and grind the beans in a meat grinder twice.

4. Add the other ingredients and mix well. Taste and correct seasoning, if needed.

5. To serve, put on a plate and smooth the surface. Garnish with pickles and olives; sprinkle with olive oil and paprika; snip parsley on top.

TAHINAH-EGGPLANT SALAD

Tahinah-Eggplant salad, which is most popular in Israel is made mainly of broiled eggplant and can be served as an appetizer, dip or first course.

For 4 Cups

2 medium eggplants
1 cup Tahinah Dip (see index)
2 tbls. lemon juice
1 garlic clove, mashed
2 tbls. chopped parsley
1½ tsp. salt
Dash pepper

1. Preheat the broiler.

2. Rinse the whole eggplants and pat dry. Do not peel. Broil eggplants 4″ away from heat, on a piece of aluminum foil. Turn the eggplants every 10 minutes to assure even cooking. Broiling time: 30 to 40 minutes.

3. Remove the eggplants from heat with a kitchen glove. Cool slightly and cut in halves. Scoop out all the flesh into a bowl. Sprinkle immediately with lemon juice, and mash thoroughly with a fork. For smooth, even texture grind in blender.

4. Cool to room temperature. Add remaining ingredients and stir until the salad is completely blended. Correct seasoning, if needed.

5. Chill in the refrigerator. Serve garnished with parsley, olives or pimientos.

VEGETARIAN 'CHICKEN LIVER'

Chopped chicken liver is a classic Jewish favorite that is easily prepared when livers are available. But it takes some imagination to produce the same taste using substitutes. In cookery, as in many other fields, Israelis had to 'make do' frequently and these creative people came up with 'chopped liver' from eggplant, which was in abundance while chickens were scarce.

1 large eggplant (2 lbs.)
½ cup flour
Oil for frying
1 medium onion
1 garlic clove
3 hard-boiled eggs
1 tsp. salt
Dash pepper

1. Peel the eggplant and cut in ½″ slices. Sprinkle with salt and let stand in the sun for about 20 minutes to draw out the bitterness.

2. Drain the liquid that accumulates and wash the slices under cold running water. Pat dry with paper towels. Sprinkle with flour.

3. Heat ½″ oil in a large skillet and fry eggplant slices until dark brown on both sides. Remove from skillet and blot excess oil with paper towels.

4. Mince the onion and garlic. Fry in the remaining oil until just golden brown. Remove from skillet.

5. Put eggplant through a meat grinder or food chopper with the onions and the eggs. Combine in a bowl. (You may chop all ingredients on a bread board with a sharp knife.) Add salt and pepper and mix well.

6. Chill in the refrigerator; garnish, before serving, with olives, parsley, sliced tomatoes and sliced hard-boiled eggs.

PITAH

Pitah is a round, flat bread with a natural 'pocket' in its center. The bread is soft and is as popular in Israel as in the Middle East from which it comes. *Pat* means Bread, in Hebrew, and *Pitah* is eaten as bread with some unusual uses: it holds small *Falafel* balls to make a neat little meal that may be eaten in the street when one is hungry. *Pitah* is also cut in small pieces to be dipped in sauces and serve as substitute for fork on some occasions. Traditionally baked very primitively on heated stones in the desert, it is now a standard item in modern bakeries. You, too, can bake your own, right in your kitchen.

For 6 8" Pitot

4 cups flour
1 tsp. salt
2 pkg. fresh yeast (0.6 oz. each)
1/8 tsp. sugar
1/4 cup warm water
1-1 1/4 cups lukewarm water
1/2 cup corn meal

1. Mix the flour with the salt.

2. Combine 1/4 cup warm water with the yeast and sugar. Let rest for 2 minutes. Stir to dissolve the yeast and let rest for 5 minutes in a warm place.

3. Make a well in the center of the flour and pour the dissolved yeast into it. Mix in some of the surrounding flour. Measure 1 cup of lukewarm water and add it gradually to the center, mixing the flour continuously. You may need an additional 1/4 cup water, if the dough is too stiff. It must be manageable: not too hard; not too wet.

4. Sprinkle some flour on your working surface and turn out the dough. Knead 40 times, pressing with the heel of your palm, pushing away from you, folding over, and pressing again. The dough should form a soft and elastic ball.

5. Wash bowl thoroughly and rinse with warm water. Dry completely and grease with salad oil. Put the dough in it, turning once to oil all over. Cover with a clean kitchen towel and let stand in a warm corner in your kitchen for 1 hour.

6. Punch down the dough, knead lightly and divide into equal parts. Knead each part lightly to form a round ball; place on a floured cookie sheet, cover with the towel and let rest 45 minutes.

7. Heat the oven to 500°F. Roll out each ball in an 8" circle. Sprinkle a large cookie sheet with corn meal and put two circles on it. Bake in the center of the oven for 5 to 7 minutes, until the *pitot* brown lightly, just a shade darker than ivory. The *pitot* will puff in the center. It is this puffing that separates the bread into two layers and forms the pocket. Remove from oven and bake two more *pitot*.

8. The *pitah* feels dry when removed from oven, but when cooled and put in a tightly closed plastic bag it regains its moisture, and thereby its softness. *Pitah* is eaten hot or warm.

9. Serve the *pitot* whole, or cut in half, which makes it easier to fill them with *falafel* and other goodies.

Note: *Pitot* freeze successfully when wrapped in freezer paper or plastic bags. For reuse put them in a brown paper bag, sprinkle with some water and heat in a slow oven.

FALAFEL

Falafel is a Middle Eastern specialty the Israelis have adopted whole-heartedly. It is a small garbanzo bean croquette, deep fried and eaten hot. Usually four or five are stuffed in a *Pitah* with salad, pickles and *Tahinah* sauce. This 'sandwich' is called *Falafel*, too, and is sold by street vendors all over Israel, the way hot dogs are sold in the United States of America. You don't need any special equipment to fix *Falafel* at home. You may prepare the mixture ahead and fry at the last minute, or even when the guests are around. The *Falafel* can then be put together as a sandwich, or piled on a large tray and served as a snack.

For 50 to 60 Falafel Croquettes

½ lb. dried garbanzo beans (1 cup)
1/3 cup cracked wheat
2 slices of wheat bread, dry
5 garlic cloves
2 tbls. parsley, chopped
3 tbls. lemon juice
1 tsp. ground cumin
¼ tsp. ground coriander
3 tsp. salt
¼ tsp. black pepper
Dash hot red pepper (optional)
2 eggs
½ cup plain bread crumbs
Oil for frying

1. Cover beans with water and soak overnight.

2. Next morning drain beans, rinse and put in a large pot. Cover with fresh water, add 2 teaspoons salt and bring to a boil; reduce heat and simmer for 1½ hours. Remove from heat and drain.

3. Soak cracked wheat in a cup of water for about 20 minutes. Soak bread separately.

4. Grind garbanzo beans in a meat grinder with garlic and parsley. Squeeze the water out of the soaked bread and grind.

5. Combine in a bowl with lemon juice, remaining salt, seasoning and eggs. Mix lightly.

6. Drain the cracked wheat and add to the mixture with half of the bread crumbs. Stir well and mix thoroughly. Add remaining bread crumbs gradually until the mixture is manageable enough to shape the *falafel.* If too soft when all bread crumbs have been used, add more to obtain proper consistency. This may be done several hours before serving. Cover with waxed paper and refrigerate.

7. To make the *falafel,* shape small balls 1″ in diameter with wet hands. Put on a tray or cookie sheet lined with waxed paper.

8. Fill a heavy 10″ or 12″ skillet with 1½″ of oil and heat to medium-high (375°). Fry about a dozen *falafels* at a time on both sides until they become deep golden brown. Remove from skillet with a slotted spoon. Put on paper towels to blot excess oil. Serve immediately.

ISRAELI VEGETABLE SALAD

There is no one recipe for an Israeli vegetable salad: the variety and quantity of the main ingredients depend on the availability of fresh, ripe vegetables in the market the day the salad is to be made. In addition, the mood or personal preferences of the cook and her family play an important role in the salad's composition. Whatever the ingredients, preparation is minimal—cutting and dressing. But the salad must be served immediately, because freshness is the secret of its good taste.

2 medium carrots
2 medium tomatoes
1 cucumber
5 radishes
3 scallions
½ head of lettuce
2 dill-pickled cucumbers
1 large bell pepper
1 tbls. chopped parsley
Juice of a whole lemon
2 tbls. salad or olive oil
1 tsp. salt
Dash pepper
Dash sugar

1. Clean all the vegetables. Peel carrots and cucumbers.

2. Use a big salad bowl and add the vegetables to it as you work: grate the carrots coarsely, cut the tomatoes in bite-size chunks, chop the radishes and scallions, shred the lettuce and dice the bell pepper and pickles. Toss and sprinkle with the lemon juice, oil and seasonings. Toss again and serve immediately.

JAFFA CHICKEN
(Photograph on page 92)

Chicken is basic to the Jewish kitchen everywhere in the world. Creative Israeli cooks have experimented with it and managed to give it unusual new flavors by combining the chicken with Jaffa oranges, raisins, Middle Eastern spices and white wine. Our version of this is a most elegant and enjoyable dish.

For 16 Pieces

3 lb. chicken, serving pieces only (2 chickens)
1½ cups orange juice
1 cup white wine
1 onion, sliced
1 celery stalk, cut up
1 carrot, sliced
1½ tsp. salt
⅛ tsp. pepper
1 tsp. paprika
3 tbls. oil
½ cup raisins
1 tsp. cumin
2 oranges, sectioned
½ tsp. grated orange peel

[97]

1. For this dish use only serving pieces: thighs, breasts, etc. Use the backs, wings and inner parts for making soup.

2. Combine orange juice, wine, vegetables and seasonings, except cumin, in a big, shallow roasting pan. Marinate the chicken pieces in it for 1 hour, turning occasionally.

3. Remove the chicken pieces from marinade and wipe dry with paper towels. Heat the oil in a large skillet and fry chicken lightly, skin-side down. Return to the marinade in the roasting pan, putting the skin side down. Add orange sections, raisins and sprinkle cumin all over. Cover tightly.

4. Bake, covered, for 1 hour at 350°F. Remove the cover and turn the chicken, skin side up. Bake, uncovered for about 30 minutes, until beautifully browned.

5. Remove the chicken, orange sections and raisins to a heated serving plate. Strain the pan juices into a small saucepan, add grated orange peel and boil juices until thick, about 7 minutes. Pour over the chicken. Serve warm.

ZUCCHINI IN TOMATO SAUCE

An adopted 'child' of the Israeli kitchen that is regarded now as a native, zucchini is prepared in many ways by the Israeli housewife. There are stuffed zucchini, zucchini baked in white sauce, a first-course zucchini salad and even a zucchini dessert. This recipe for zucchini in tomato sauce is equally delicious hot or cold.

```
1 large onion
2 tbls. olive oil
2 tbls. salad oil
2 lb. green firm zucchini
1 6-oz. can tomato paste
1 cup water
1 beef bouillon cube
1 garlic clove, finely minced
1 tsp. salt
Dash pepper
Dash thyme
2 tbls. parsley, snipped
```

1. Chop the onion and fry in oil in a large shallow saucepan.

2. Wash zucchini. Do not peel if the skin looks fresh and smooth; simply scrub thoroughly and remove stems. If the skin has scars, peel. Cut the zucchini in 1″ chunks and add to saucepan.

3. Sauté lightly with the onions. Add the tomato paste, water, bouillon cube, garlic and seasonings.

4. Bring to a boil, then reduce heat and simmer very gently for 1½ hours.

5. To serve, sprinkle the dish with snipped parsley.

FRESH FRUIT DESSERT

Fresh fruits are a favorite of the Israelis. When a variety of fruit is combined in a salad the result is delicious and colorful, yet interestingly enough, such salads are eaten only at the end of the meal, and are regarded as a sweet, satisfying dessert. Citrus fruit is a 'must' in any Israeli fresh fruit salad.

```
1 grapefruit
3 oranges
2 tart apples
2 pears
1 cup raisins
3 cups orange juice
1 tbls. lemon juice
2 tbls. sugar
```

1. Peel oranges and grapefruit. Clean and core apples and pears.

2. Section the grapefruit and carefully remove the membranes. Put in a salad bowl, preferably glass, to let the beauty of the fruits show through.

3. Remove the white parts from the oranges and slice thinly crosswise. Remove seeds and add to the bowl. Dice apples and pears in small cubes and add to the bowl with remaining ingredients. Mix lightly. Cover with waxed paper and refrigerate. This salad can be prepared several hours ahead. Serve cold.

IX

LAG BA'OMER: SUMMER
COOKING GOES OUTDOORS

L AG BA'OMER is a one-day holiday commemorating the bravery of Jewish soldiers and students. Its roots may be traced back in ancient Israel about eighteen centuries, to the time when a small army led by Bar Kochba dared to revolt against the legions of the Roman Empire. They sought to regain freedom and independence and were willing to sacrifice everything to achieve it. Bar Kochba (the son of a star, in Hebrew) was assisted by Rabbi Akiba, a great scholar of the time. The Rabbi's support was more than moral: he and his many students participated actively in the revolt, fighting side-by-side with the soldiers for their right to live in accordance with Jewish culture and heritage.

The holiday is celebrated as an outdoors day. Schools close and children join their teachers in parks and fields for sports, games and races. Some children arm themselves with primitive bows and arrows and have great fun. The Israeli army conducts sharpshooting competitions and Israeli students have chosen *Lag Ba'Omer* as the national students' day. With nightfall, big bonfires and small campfires are lit; youngsters and adults gather around them to dance and sing late into the night.

The bonfires on *Lag Ba'Omer* mark the beginning of the outdoor cooking season. Cookouts can be spontaneous, or planned meticulously, but they have one thing in common: an easy-going informality. Rigid laws of etiquette disappear, along with ties and jackets; guests and hosts relax and enjoy themselves.

Warm Weather Cookout

(Photograph on page 100)

This outdoor meal can be as informal as you like: you and your guests can dress casually, even go barefoot; you can use paper or plastic dishes and utensils and forget the seating arrangements (they are non-existent). Let everyone share the chores as well as the fun.

Our cookout meal is composed of easy-to-prepare, make-ahead dishes: a zesty *Tahinah* Dip is served as the guests gather. This Mediterranean sauce goes well with the *Shishlik* and *Kabab* that are part of the Mixed Grill, and are also of Middle Eastern origin. Serve both with *Pitah*, a round flat bread with a 'pocket' in it. You can fill this pocket with meat, salad and *Tahinah* dip, thereby eliminating the need for plates and forks. (*Pitah* bread can be purchased at stores specializing in Middle Eastern products. Or, you can make it at home. See index for recipe.)

WARM WEATHER COOKOUT. The entire outdoor meal is shown in this picture. From left to right: the HOMEMADE LEMONADE (recipe on page 103), MINI RELISH TRAYS (recipe on page 102), BAKED POTATOES in aluminum foil (recipe on page 103), and the MIXED GRILL skewers (recipe on page 102). Surrounding the meat are the various sauces and dips. From the top are the BARBEQUE SAUCE (recipe on page 102), PICKLE DIP (recipe on page 101), and a plate of hot pickles and TAHINAH (recipe on page 101). In the background, between the watermelon and lemonade glasses, is PITAH bread (recipe on page 96), the flat round bread used in this meal.

As starchy dishes we have Baked Potatoes and Baked Corn. Outdoor meals tend to perk up appetites and these two vegetables will be eagerly eaten. However, since you know your guests and their appetites, you may decide to include just one on your menu. To arrange the serving table, set out plates with pickled vegetables, the Mini-Relish 'Tray', Barbecue Sauce, *Pitah* bread, Lemonade and fruit. Let the guests help themselves; you will all enjoy the outdoor meal, whether it takes place on the beach, in the park or in your own back yard.

MENU
(planned for 6 to 8)
Pickle Dip*
Tahinah Dip*
Mini Relish 'Trays'*
Mixed Grill*
Meat Marinade*
Barbeque Sauce*
Pitah bread (see index)
Baked Potatoes*
Baked Corn*
Fruit
Homemade Lemonade*
Recipe given

PICKLE DIP
(Photograph on page 100)

A tangy sauce-spread to use on soft buns or inside round *Pitah* bread. It perks up the food that it is served with.

> 1 cup mayonnaise
> ½ cup finely chopped pickles
> 1 tbls. dehydrated onion flakes
> 2 tbls. mustard
> Dash pepper

1. Mix all ingredients well. Keep refrigerated until meal time.

TAHINAH DIP
(Photograph on page 100)

Tahinah is a very appetizing, velvety dip made of sesame-seed paste, mixed with water and lemon juice. Turn it into a sauce and use it to dress salads, too. The paste can be purchased in health food stores.

For 1 2/3 Cups
1 Cup Tahinah (sesame seed paste)
2/3 cup water
1/3 cup lemon juice
2 garlic cloves, mashed
1 tsp. salt
⅛ tsp. pepper
1 tbls. snipped parsley
¼ tsp. paprika

1. Measure 1 cup of *Tahinah* paste in a medium bowl. Add the water in a slow stream stirring continuously. The paste may turn white and separate. Do not worry, just stir in the lemon juice and the paste will become smooth and velvety. (Because of differences between brands of *Tahinah* paste you may find that you need to add a little more water, or an additional tablespoon of paste. The end result should have a consistency of mayonnaise.)

2. Add the mashed garlic, salt, pepper and parsley. Mix well. Put in a serving bowl and sprinkle with paprika.

MINI RELISH 'TRAYS'
(Photograph on page 100)

Easy to make relishes that add zest to the barbecue meal and bright accent to your table. Green bell peppers serve as 'trays' for fresh vegetables, olives and pickles.

For 4 Relish Trays

4 bell peppers
1 big carrot
4 green onions
4 cherry tomatoes
1 8-oz. can of green olives
1 4-oz. can of ripe black olives

1. Wash the peppers. Cut off stems and a bit of the pepper to make a 'dish'. Cut out the inedible parts and seeds with a sharp, small knife.

2. Clean and peel the carrot. Divide in fourths, cutting lengthwise with a ruffled vegetable cutter. Clean the tomatoes and green onions. Remove the outer membranes of the onions and cut off any blemished green ends.

3. Fill each pepper with the 2 kinds of olives. Tuck in a carrot stick and onion and garnish with a cherry tomato.

MIXED GRILL
(Photograph on page 100)

A variety of grilled meats pleases everyone. Prepare *Shishlik* from marinated cubed beef or lamb; *Kabab* from ground meat; chicken livers and cocktail franks. Put them on skewers, brush with barbecue sauce and grill them to perfection.

1 lb. beef steak or tender lamb
1 lb. ground meat
½ lb. chicken liver
½ lb. cocktail franks
2 bell peppers
2 onions
½ basket cherry tomatoes
3 tsp. finely chopped parsley

1. Start the *shishlik* at least 4 hours before grilling. You may even do it the night before: cut the steak or lamb in 1″ cubes, place in a shallow glass or enamel pan and pour on marinade (recipe follows). Cover and refrigerate for 4 hours or overnight.

2. Make the *kababs* early on the day of cookout. Mix the ground meat with parsley and shape in 16 thin, elongated patties about 2″ long. Cover and refrigerate.

3. Cut the onions and peppers in bite-sized chunks, place in separate bowls, cover and refrigerate.

4. Prepare barbeque sauce (recipe follows).

5. Shortly before grilling time, quarter the chicken livers and assemble the mixed grill: put each kind of meat on a skewer alternating with vegetables. For 8 people you will need 16 metal skewers or 32 small wooden ones. (Be sure to put skewers through the center of the meat to prevent falling off.) You may, of course, arrange different pieces of meat on one skewer.

6. Brush the *kababs* and franks with barbeque sauce, and moisten the *shishliks* with the Meat Marinade. Sprinkle seasoned salt on the chicken livers, and grill for about 7 minutes on each side. You can also prepare these meats under the broiler in your kitchen.

MEAT MARINADE

This marinade tenderizes less expensive meat cuts and improves the better ones. Marinating is not a rapid process, so plan on doing it several hours before the barbeque to let the meat absorb the flavor of the marinating ingredients. Use the marinade juices for basting the meat while on the fire.

¼ cup salad or olive oil
¾ cup vinegar
1 tsp. powdered mustard
2 tsp. sugar
1 tsp. salt
¼ tsp. pepper
2 tsp. soy sauce
3 garlic cloves
2 tbls. chopped onion

1. Mix all ingredients together. Put the meat in a shallow dish big enough to hold all of the pieces and pour marinade over. Refrigerate for several hours or overnight.

2. Turn the meat in the marinade occasionally, during this period, to assure even distribution of the flavors.

3. Barbeque as directed. The change in the taste will be unmistakeable.

BARBEQUE SAUCE
(Photograph on page 100)

This piquant sauce does more than add flavor and color to the meats; it moistens them and prevents their drying out during cooking. The result is meat that is tender, juicy and very appetizing. Prepare the sauce and brush it on the meat before and during the broiling. Our sauce is appropriate for many kinds of meat: steak, *kababs, shisliks,* poultry and hamburgers. If you have marinated the meat you don't have to use the sauce.

For About 1 Cup Sauce

1 onion
½ cup ketchup
¼ cup vinegar
2 tsp. salt
½ tsp. pepper
1 tbls. honey
1 tbls. prepared mustard
Drop hot pepper sauce (optional)

1. Chop the onion in very small dice. Combine with ketchup, vinegar, salt, pepper, and honey in a medium saucepan.

2. Cook over medium-low heat for 15 minutes. Stir occasionally.

3. Remove from heat, add mustard and hot pepper sauce. Use immediately or store in a closed jar in the refrigerator.

BAKED POTATOES
(Photograph on page 100)

Baked potatoes will go very well with an outdoor meal. Bake them in the oven, on your barbeque, or even in an open fire when you go camping. Baking time is quite long, so plan ahead.

8 medium baking potatoes (4 lb.)
8 pieces of aluminum foil
¼ cup oil
4-6 tbls. margarine
2 tbls. snipped chives
Salt
Pepper

1. Choose nice looking potatoes. They should be of equal size to cook evenly and be ready at the same time. Clean and scrub potatoes but do not peel. Rub with some of the oil and put each potato in the center of an aluminum foil square big enough to cover it completely.

2. Put the wrapped potatoes in a 400°F oven or on your barbecue. Baking time is about 1½ hours.

3. When the potatoes are tender remove from heat with a kitchen mitten to protect your hand. Roll each potato on a flat surface, pressing gently

with your covered hand. This will make the inside soft and crumbly, as if it was whipped.

4. Use a sharp knife to cut each potato through the foil wrapping. Make two straight incisions, crossing each other. Fold back the potato peel and foil to create a pretty design (see picture).

5. Put 1 tablespoon margarine in the opening and mix with the potato flesh, using a fork. Sprinkle with salt, pepper and chopped chives. Add more margarine, if needed.

BAKED CORN

A delicious, satisfying side dish for an outdoor meal. Use very fresh corn or else blanch older corn in hot water for 15 minutes then finish baking in the oven or on the barbeque.

8 ears sweet, fresh corn
8 pieces aluminum foil
2 tbls. margarine
Salt

1. Shuck corn, remove all silk and rinse well. Put each ear on a piece of aluminum foil. Wrap the foil around the corn and twist the ends, as if wrapping a candy. This will let some steam escape and the corn will roast rather than steam.

2. Bake the wrapped corn in a 400°F oven for 30 minutes, turning them occasionally. When the corn is tender to your touch serve hot with margarine and a sprinkling of salt.

HOMEMADE LEMONADE
(Photograph on page 100)

Accompany your outdoor meal with tangy and cool lemonade. Use fresh lemons, for a true, natural flavor, and garnish the tall glasses with round lemon slices.

8 cups cold water
1¼ cups lemon juice
1 cup sugar
Ice cubes
1 lemon, thinly sliced

1. Squeeze enough fresh lemons to make 1¼ cups juice. Strain it through a fine sieve into a pitcher. Add sugar and ½ cup water. Stir until sugar dissolves. Add the cold water and ice cubes, and stir well.

2. Choose the 8 best looking lemon slices, and reserve them for garnishing the glasses. Put the rest into the pitcher.

Nuts, cherries, strawberries, chocolate sauce, and crushed fruit are the essential ingredients for establishing your private Ice Cream Parlor. You can use them when you serve the dishes shown in the picture. At the back is the ICE CREAM CAKE, decorated with whipped cream rosettes (recipe on page 109) and the ICE CREAM FRUITY DRINK (recipe on page 109) which is loaded with strawberries. In front is the homemade version of a classic BANANA SPLIT (recipe on page 109).

X

SHAVUOT: DAIRY DISHES FOR YOUR DELIGHT

LITERALLY, *Shavuot* means 'Weeks', and stands for the fact that this holiday is celebrated seven weeks after Passover. It is a two-fold holiday that brings together culture and agriculture. Tradition has it that the Ten Commandments and the *Torah* were given to Moses on Mount Sinai, on *Shavuot*. This puts *Shavuot* in the first rank among Jewish holidays, since the *Torah* contains the essence of Jewish law, principles and history.

Shavuot is also an agricultural holiday that was celebrated in ancient Israel. The seven weeks between Passover and *Shavuot* was the grain harvesting season. With the advent of *Shavuot* came the beginning of the early fruit harvesting. In those days, people would go to Jerusalem on their third Pilgrimage of the year to the Temple—after *Succot* and Passover. They would bring presents of new fruits *(Bikkurim)*, from their orchards, vineyards and fields. These presents were a selection of the Seven Kinds *(Shivat Haminim)*, for which the Land of Israel is famed: grapes, figs, pomegranates, olive oil, honey, wheat and barley.

The customs of *Shavuot* are tied to the double meaning of the holiday. Homes, classrooms and synagogues are decorated with green branches, flowers and fruits. Today school children in Israel commemorate the *Bikkurim* Pilgrimage by bringing baskets of fruits and flowers to be donated for worthy causes. The book of Ruth, which provides a beautiful description of the harvest during Biblical times, is read on *Shavuot*. There is no doubt, on this holiday, of the strong link between *Torah* and the Harvest; the Book and the Land.

It is customary to eat dairy dishes on *Shavuot*. There are many folk stories to explain this tradition. Some say that before receiving the *Torah* on *Shavuot* the Jews abstained from all meat dishes as personal sacrifice. Others say that the *Torah* is as sweet and as nourishing as milk and honey to those who study it; therefore, the holiday on which the *Torah* was given is celebrated with dairy foods. Let the real reason be what it may, we have gained marvelous dishes as a result of this custom.

Cheese cakes, cheese pies and other dishes with no trace of meat in them comprise *Shavuot's* array of delicacies and recipes. Some are given in this chapter. You will find that dairy dishes can be exciting and exceptionally good. Ours, ranging from the seasoned to the sweet, include Heavenly Cheese Omelet, *Kosher Quicke*, Low-Fat *Blintzes* and a Gala Cheese Cake. All can be ranked high on any gourmet's list and are fit for distinguished entertaining at easy-going brunches or elegant little lunches. Some can be prepared ahead and some need last minute operations to reach the peak of their goodness. Either way, they are worth your trying. Please note that we use low-fat ingredients in part of the recipes. This is our way of letting you eat your cake and . . . also keep your figure.

We also include in this chapter hand-picked recipes for Ice Cream Treats. Use them to create ice cream cakes, drinks and desserts that are very appropriate on *Shavuot,* the dairy holiday, but delicious at any time. For informal get-togethers we have a complete menu for a Midnight Pizza Party that complies with the holiday's customs.

HEAVENLY CHEESE OMELET

A cheese omelet to serve proudly at a small luncheon. It has a gourmet touch, yet is quick, easy and fun to prepare.

For 2 Persons

4 eggs
¼ tsp. cream of tartar
½ tsp. salt
2 tbls. butter
½ cup grated Cheddar cheese
4 tbls. sour cream
1 tbls. chopped chives

Please read the whole recipe before starting!

1. Preheat broiler. Put an oven-proof skillet on top of the stove on low heat and melt the butter. Tilt the skillet to grease sides as well as the bottom.

2. Separate the eggs. Whip the whites with the cream of tartar until stiff but not dry.

3. In a separate bowl, whip the yolks together with 2 tablespoons cold water and the salt until yolks are very pale.

4. Fold the yolks into the whites very gently. The whole mixture will have a pale yellow color. Pour it gently into the skillet. Fry for 3 minutes or until the bottom begins to brown.

5. Put the skillet under a hot broiler for about 5 minutes. The omelet should puff and have a golden color on top. Remove from broiler.

6. Run a knife along the edges of the skillet to loosen the omelet. Cut omelet down the middle which will help you fold it. Sprinkle the grated cheese along the cut and fold over. Garnish with sour cream and chives. Serve immediately.

KOSHER QUICHE

A flavorful salted cheese pie for *Shavuot* that is a favorite of Sephardic Jews, who can't accept the idea of sweetened cheese. You can serve this dish at luncheon and you will find it great for entertaining.

For 4 to 6 Servings

Crust:
2 cups flour
½ tsp. salt
4 oz. butter (½ cup)
5 tbls. cold water

Cheese filling:
1 cup milk
½ cup cream
2 eggs
½ tsp. salt
Pinch of pepper and nutmeg
5 oz. Swiss cheese, grated
1 tbls. butter

1. Cut the butter into the flour, and mix with your hands until pieces are the size of small peas.

2. Add salt and water and knead until you have a smooth ball. Cover with waxed paper and refrigerate for 1 hour. Meanwhile prepare filling.

3. Measure the milk and cream into a bowl. Add the eggs, the seasonings, the cheese and combine. Stir very well. Set aside.

4. Roll out the pastry dough, and line a 9″ pie pan with it. Trim the edges and pour the filling in the center. Cut the butter in small pieces and dot the top.

5. Bake in a 375°F oven for 30 minutes or until the top is browned and puffed.

MY FAVORITE LOW-FAT BLINTZES

Blintzes are old favorites in Jewish cuisine. They are very thin egg pancakes rolled and filled with various fillings. One can trace their origin to the French kitchen because the similarity to the delicate crêpes is very obvious. Our *blintzes* for the holiday of *Shavuot* are filled with sweetened cheese and garnished with fruits. Serve them at lunchtime or for brunch. Please note that artificial sweetners, low-fat milk and cottage cheese are used to cut down the calories, but not the taste.

For 8 Blintzes

Batter:
5 tbls. flour
2 large eggs
½ tsp. salt
1 tsp. vanilla
1 cup low-fat milk
1½ tbls. salad oil

Cheese filling:
4 tbls. cottage cheese
2 tbls. sugar (or equivalent in non-caloric sweetner)
1 tsp. vanilla
/4 tsp. grated lemon rind
¼ tsp. grated orange rind
½ cup frozen blueberries, thawed
2 tbls. blueberry jam, optional

1. Put the flour in a medium bowl or a large measuring cup, and add the milk in a slow stream, stirring constantly. There should be no lumps. Add the eggs, salt, vanilla and 1 tablespoon oil. Mix very well. For a more homogenized batter you can use your blender. The batter should be quite liquid, like heavy cream; if it is too thick add more milk.

2. Mix all the filling ingredients, and let sit outside the refrigerator, until you are ready to use.

3. Use a teflon-coated small skillet about 6″ in diameter. Coat the skillet lightly with oil (you still have ½ tablespoon), or put a drop of oil on a paper napkin and grease skillet with this.

4. Heat the skillet on a high flame. When a drop of water starts to 'dance' on the surface, ladle in about 2 tablespoons of the batter. Turn skillet so that batter spreads evenly over the bottom. Cook until batter looks dry and the edges pull away from skillet walls.

5. Turn the skillet over a plate and, with a strong knock, let the thin *blintze* fall on the plate. It will be easier if the plate is set upside down on the table.

6. Continue preparing the *blintzes* in this fashion until all the batter is used. Grease the skillet lightly, occasionally.

7. Put 2 teaspoons of filling in one end of a *blintze;* roll and fold the sides around the filling to make a long envelope. When all *blintzes* are filled and rolled, heat in a skillet.

8. Serve hot, and pass the jam.

SWEET CINNAMON NOODLES

The following is a typical example of a dish that is hearty, tasty, yet simple. The main ingredients are buttered noodles, cottage cheese, sugar and cinnamon. Low-cost materials that are worth a million . . .

For 4 to 6 Servings
1 7-oz. pkg. broad noodles
2 oz. butter (¼ cup)
1 cup cottage cheese
4 tbls. sugar
2 tsp. cinnamon

1. Cook the noodles in a large pot of boiling, salted water for about 8 minutes. Do not overcook. Put the noodles in a colander, rinse with hot water and drain. Turn into a large bowl (preferably warm).

2. Melt the butter and pour over the hot noodles. Quickly add the cheese, sugar and cinnamon. Toss all the ingredients and combine thoroughly. Serve immediately, while still hot.

GALA CHEESE CAKE

The Gala Cheese Cake here is delicate and rich. Follow the directions carefully, and you won't regret it.

1½ cups cookie crumbs
4 oz. butter (½ cup)
2 tsp. grated lemon rind
4 cups cottage cheese, whipped
½ cup flour
1 cup sugar
4 eggs
1 tsp. vanilla extract

1. Preheat the oven to 350°F. Pulverize enough cookies (wafers, cornflakes, or graham crackers) to make 1½ cups crumbs. Melt the butter and add to the crumbs with 1 teaspoon lemon rind. Combine thoroughly.

2. Line the bottom of a 9″ springform pan with waxed paper. Grease the sides very well. Spread the buttered crumbs on the bottom of the pan, tilt it and press part of the crumbs along the sides, around lower edge.

3. Put the cheese in a mixing bowl with the sugar, flour, egg yolks, vanilla and the remaining teaspoon lemon rind. Mix gently, but well.

4. Whip the egg whites until they are stiff. Fold them gently into cheese.

5. Pour into springform and bake for 1 hour without opening the door. Turn off the heat and let the cake cool in oven for another hour. The cake will puff while baking, but will set when it cools. Cool in the refrigerator for at least another 2 hours.

6. To unmold the cake, run a knife around edge of pan to loosen. Remove the sides of the pan, leave the bottom for added support. Put on a nice cake platter.

7. Serve the cake cold, with whipped cream, if you like.

Ice Cream Treats

It is believed that ice cream originated in China. Some say that Marco Polo brought it to Europe; others believe that Richard the Lion-Hearted got the recipe from Salah Addin in the Twelfth Century. Italians take the credit for refining ice cream and Americans are proud of mass producing it so that everyone can enjoy it. Indeed, ice cream was a treat reserved for royalty until comparatively recent times; before modern refrigeration only they could afford 'natural' ice boxes on their estates. The ice box was just that: a whole hill with a cave dug in its northern side. In winter the cave was filled with chunks of ice from frozen rivers and lakes, then insulated with hay to keep the ice through the summer. If the owner desired ice cream his servants would go to the cave at night, to keep the sun's rays out, fill a bucket with ice and salt and set a smaller bucket in it. The small bucket contained cream, sugar and fresh fruit purée and was hand-turned to velvety smoothness for royal pleasure.

Although the principles of ice cream making are the same today—whipping and chilling simultaneously—methods have progressed to the point where it is an inexpensive treat that is popular with all ages and welcome any season. There is practically no limit on the ways you can serve ice cream, whether you make your own or use commercial brands. You will find recipes for some ice cream parlor favorites in this chapter, plus one for a delicious Homemade Ice Cream you can make in your refrigerator.

Ice Cream Cake
Banana Split
Ice Cream Fruity Drink
Hot Fudge Sundae
Homemade Ice Cream

ICE CREAM CAKE
(Photograph on page 104)

An ice cream cake is a good solution to an entertainment problem. The cake can be in the freezer waiting for the guests. Master the basic 'baking' techniques then you can create variations of your own.

Our cake is made of chocolate ice cream with vanilla ice cream in center. It rests on a layer of wafer crumbs, and is garnished with whipped cream rosettes. Please note that there is a waiting period between the steps while the layers harden, so allow plenty of time for setting.

1 pint vanilla ice cream
1 pint chocolate ice cream
¾ cup vanilla wafers' crumbs
3 tbls. butter
½ cup whipping cream
2 tbls. confectioners' sugar
1 8-oz. can peaches, drained
Candied cherries
4 green marmalade candies

1. Chill a 4-cup melon mold in the freezer. Set your freezer to the coldest point while preparing the cake; return to normal once the cake freezes.

2. Put half the chocolate ice cream in a bowl and stir vigorously with a wooden spoon until it softens a little. Quickly put the softened ice cream in the chilled mold and press to the edges to cover the inside completely with an even layer. Add more ice cream, if needed; if it slips and does not stick to the sides of the mold, put the mold in freezer for 30 minutes, or until the ice cream hardens, and you can lift it to form a smooth lining. Freeze the mold until this layer is completely hard.

3. Soften the vanilla ice cream the same as the chocolate. Put inside the chocolate layer, pressing lightly to smooth surface. Freeze for 10 minutes.

4. Meantime, melt the butter and combine with the wafer crumbs. Remove mold from freezer and sprinkle an even layer of crumbs. (When cake is ready this will be the bottom layer.) Wrap in waxed paper and freeze overnight.

5. About an hour before serving time whip the cream until fluffy and holds its shape. Sweeten with sugar at the last stages of whipping. Fit a pastry bag with a large star tube and fill with whipped cream. Unmold the 'cake': wet a towel with hot water, invert mold on a chilled platter and cover with hot towel. Tilt mold until cake slips out.

6. Press the pastry bag to push out whipped cream rosettes on top and around sides of cake. Return to freezer.

7. Just before serving, arrange the fruits and candy around the cake in a nice design.

BANANA SPLIT
(Photograph on page 104)

A big, ripe banana embraces three ice cream scoops of different flavors, all surrounded by a river of chocolate sauce and topped with mountains of whipped cream peaked with chopped nuts, candied cherries and peaches. This is the unbeatable 'banana split' and you can do it at home!

For Each Serving

1 ripe banana
1 tbls. lemon juice
3 ice cream scoops, assorted flavors
2 canned peaches
4 strawberries
Chocolate sauce
Whipped cream
Chopped nuts
Candied cherry

1. Halve the banana lengthwise and dip in lemon juice to prevent discoloration. Chop the nuts and cut the peaches into small pieces.

2. Put the banana halves in an oval plate. Arrange the ice cream scoops between parts of banana or on top of them. Put the strawberries on one scoop, the peaches on another. Top the center scoop with whipped cream. Pour the chocolate sauce around the banana. Sprinkle with chopped nuts and garnish with a cherry.

ICE CREAM FRUITY DRINK
(Photograph on page 104)

Delightful to have on a hot summer day!

For 2 Drinks

2/3 cup milk
2 scoops vanilla ice cream
1 cup mashed fruit (strawberries, peaches or apricots)
2 tsp. sugar

1. Mash the fruit in the blender. Add milk. sugar and ice cream. Blend for 10 seconds. The milk shake should be thick and smooth.

2. Pour into tall glasses. Garnish with more fruit and add another scoop of ice cream if you wish.

HOT FUDGE SUNDAE

This sundae is topped with hot fudge that you can prepare yourself. It may interest you to know that this delicious dish got its name from 'Sunday', the only day in the week on which puritan American pioneers allowed themselves to indulge. You too can live a little, and not 'only on Sundays'.

For Each Sundae

2 scoops ice cream
Hot fudge sauce
Whipped cream
Chopped walnuts
1 cherry
1 wafer

1. Put the ice cream scoops on a dessert plate and pour some hot fudge over them. Top with a big dollop of whipped cream and sprinkle on chopped walnuts. Crown with a red cherry, put a wafer along side.

HOT FUDGE SAUCE

For 4 to 6 Portions

2 tbls. butter
2 oz. unsweetened chocolate
½ cup sugar
¾ cup light cream
1 tsp. vanilla extract

1. Melt the butter and the unsweetened chocolate in a small saucepan, on medium heat. Stir constantly with a wooden spoon.

2. Add the cream and sugar. Cook and continue stirring for another 4 or 5 minutes. The sauce should be very smooth and velvety. Add the vanilla extract and stir.

3. Cool the sauce a little, but serve it warm.

The warm sauce adds to the pleasure of eating cold ice cream.

4. Keep leftover sauce in the refrigerator. Warm over hot water before using again.

HOMEMADE ICE CREAM

There is something very special about homemade ice cream. It is sweeter, richer and creamier than the best commercial brands, even though the texture is somewhat different. You will feel a sense of pride and pleasure when you succeed in producing at home a dish that you normally would buy. Once you master the basic technique you will be able to make many flavors of ice cream, and in no time you will have your own 'Specialty of the House', without having to buy any special equipment or ingredients.

For 4 to 6 Servings

1 cup whipping cream
2 egg yolks
½ cup sugar
1 1-lb. can peaches, drained
½ tsp. grated lemon rind

1. Bring the cream and ¼ cup sugar to a slow boil in a stainless steel pot. When the sugar dissolves, remove from heat.

2. Beat the egg yolks and remaining sugar in a bowl until the yolks are pale yellow. Add the very hot cream in a slow stream and beat well. Cool.

3. Purée enough peaches in a blender to make 1 cup. Add to the cooled cream mixture together with the lemon rind. Reserve remaining peaches for garnish.

4. Pour the mixture into ice-cube trays leaving cube dividers in the trays. Freeze 3 to 4 hours.

5. Put frozen cream cubes in a bowl and beat thoroughly with an electric beater until fluffy. Do not let mixture melt completely. Return to freezer. For fluffier ice cream repeat the operation after 4 more hours, and then freeze overnight in a covered dish.

6. To serve, scoop out the ice cream, put in dessert dishes, garnish with reserved fruit and additional whipped cream.

Midnight Pizza Party

The curtain falls. The theater goes dark. The show was good and everybody is pleased. But a small pang of hunger is felt. It is too late for a heavy meal and too early for breakfast. You crave something crisp, hot and tasty; something you and your friends can munch on while discussing the show.

By planning ahead you can be the one to fulfill the group's wish for that 'something'. Without too much effort on your part you can say confidently 'let's go to my place', because you have pizza ready to go in the oven the minute you walk in the door; salad and dessert are all set in the refrigerator and cookies are in the jar.

A midnight party can be as informal as you wish; no need to use your most complicated recipes or your best china. The main idea is to prepare dishes whose main charm, besides good taste, is their ability to wait for you. Everything on our menu can be prepared ahead and given minor last-minute touches in a spotless kitchen while your friends look on admiringly.

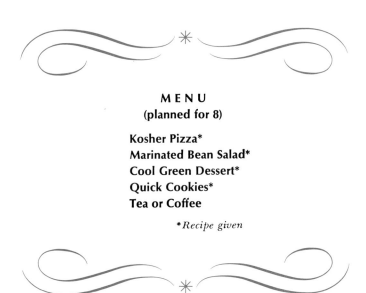

MENU
(planned for 8)

Kosher Pizza*
Marinated Bean Salad*
Cool Green Dessert*
Quick Cookies*
Tea or Coffee

*Recipe given

MIDNIGHT PIZZA PARTY. The hub of this party is KOSHER PIZZA (recipe on page 113). It is preceded by MARINATED BEAN SALAD (recipe on page 113), and followed by the COOL GREEN DESSERT (recipe on page 113). QUICK COOKIES (recipe on page 114) accompany the hot coffee to complete this party.

KOSHER PIZZA
(Photograph on page 112)

Homemade Pizza is a special treat for family as well as friends. The dough is fragrant and crisp, the topping is a tempting combination of anchovies, spicy sauce and melted cheese. It's quite easy to do, too.

Dough:
1 cake fresh yeast (0.6 oz.)
¾ cup lukewarm water
1½ cup flour
1 tsp. salt
2 tbls. salad oil

Sauce and toppings:
1 6-oz. can tomato paste
1 clove garlic, mashed
2 tbls. olive oil
½ tsp. salt
Dash pepper
½ tsp. thyme
1 tsp. oregano
4 oz. Cheddar cheese
1 2-oz. can flat filet of anchovies
10 black olives

1. Combine the yeast with the water, let rest for 5 minutes, then add the flour and salt. Knead lightly. Add the oil and knead until a smooth, elastic dough forms. About 8 minutes. (You may have to sprinkle a little more flour while kneading.)

2. Put in a large, slightly greased bowl. Cover and let rise in a warm place 1 hour, or until double in volume. While dough rises prepare the goodies to go on the pizza.

3. Grate the cheese coarsely. Mix tomato paste with ⅔ cup water, garlic, oil, salt, pepper and thyme. Drain anchovies. Set aside.

4. After an hour, turn dough out on a floured surface and knead about 1 minute. Roll in a 12″ circle and place on a greased baking sheet or special round pizza pan. Pinch the edges of the dough so it will stand up slightly.

5. Spread the tomato sauce on the dough leaving the edges clear. Arrange anchovies and olives so that every guest will have his share, and sprinkle the cheese on top evenly. You can stop at this point and refrigerate pizza until baking time.

6. To bake, preheat the oven to 450°F. Sprinkle the oregano and bake for 20 minutes. The pizza is ready when cheese is melted and dough is nicely browned. Serve hot.

MARINATED BEAN SALAD
(Photograph on page 112)

Marinated beans make a piquant salad that takes about two minutes, and can be prepared several hours before serving. Make this in advance to allow the flavors to blend.

1 1-lb. can green beans
1 1-lb. can wax beans
1 4-oz. can pimiento, sliced
2 hard-boiled eggs, quartered
8 black olives
1 small lettuce

Salad dressing:
¼ cup salad or olive oil
¼ cup vinegar
⅛ tsp. black pepper
½ tsp. salt
⅛ tsp. powdered mustard

1. Mix all the salad dressing ingredients in a cup. Stir vigorously with a fork for 1 whole minute until smooth and thickened.

2. Drain the beans and put each kind in a separate bowl. Pour salad dressing over, toss and refrigerate until serving time.

3. To serve, arrange whole lettuce leaves on a platter. Place the marinated beans attractively on them. Garnish with the red pimiento, black olives and quarters of the hard-boiled eggs.

COOL GREEN DESSERT
(Photograph on page 112)

This dessert needs no last-minute attention. It keeps its shimmering green cool in the refrigerator while you 'do your thing'.

For 8 Servings
2 3-oz. pkg. (lemon or lime) gelatin
2 cups boiling water
1½ cups cold water
1½ cups cut up strawberries
1 orange
8 4-oz. metal molds or pyrex cups

1. Dissolve the gelatin in boiling water. Add the cold water and divide between two bowls. Refrigerate one until completely set; cool the other at room temperature.

2. Whip the completely set gelatin with an electric mixer until light, fluffy and bright in color.

3. As soon as gelatin in other bowl has become

thick, but not fully set, add strawberries, reserving eight slices for garnishing.

4. Fill molds or cups halfway with whipped gelatin, and spoon the fruit-filled gelatin over it. Refrigerate at least 4 hours. Unmold and serve on individual dessert plates, garnished with orange sections and a slice of strawberry. Refrigerate until needed.

5. To unmold; dip each mold in hot water 10 seconds; run tip of knife around edges. Invert on dessert plate, shake gently until dessert slides down.

6. To prepare orange garnish, peel orange, remove membranes of each section, then cut crosswise in 1/4″ slices.

QUICK COOKIES
(Photograph on page 112)

The mixer does almost all of the work for you with these cookies. No rolling or cutting, just push them through a cookie press. They keep well in an airtight jar or in the freezer. That is, of course, if they are not eaten right away.

For 50 Cookies

8 oz. butter (1 cup)
1 cup sugar
1 egg
2 tsp. vanilla extract
2 tbls. milk
2½ cups flour
1½ tsp. baking powder
¼ tsp. salt

1. Preheat the oven to 450°F.

2. In a large mixing bowl whip the butter and sugar until very light and fluffy, for about 5 minutes. Add the egg and continue beating. Add the milk and beat again.

3. Mix the flour, salt and baking powder together. Add to the butter, beating at low speed. When mixed well put the dough in a cookie press.

4. Press out the cookies on a teflon cookie sheet, leaving about 1″ between, since they spread in the oven. You can also drop the dough from a teaspoon, but a press makes nicer, more even, cookies.

5. Bake in a hot oven for about 8 to 10 minutes. The cookies are done when very light brown on the edge and almost white in the center. Watch them carefully if you don't want to have burnt cookies. You will find that the second and third batches need less time in the oven so the baking is completed very quickly.

6. Remove the cookies from the oven. Lift off pan with a spatula. Cool on a rack. The cookies are soft when warm but will get crisp very shortly.

XI
SHABBAT: PEACEFUL FEASTS

P EACE, REST AND RELAXATION characterize *Shabbat,* the seventh day of each week. In the Jewish tradition no work is allowed on this day and all regular activities come to a halt, providing a complete change-of-pace. One enjoys calmness and harmony rather than the tension and trouble of regular working days.

Shabbat begins on Friday afternoon as the sun sets and ends when the first stars shine on Saturday night. In many rituals *Shabbat* is regarded as a Queen that comes to dwell with the family for one day and, indeed, *Shabbat* is welcomed like Royalty. The preparations start well in advance, with the house being cleaned and shopping and cooking planned to be completed before sunset. The table is nicely set and the family dresses with particular care for the occasion. The atmosphere in the Jewish traditional home is at once festive and serene.

The lady of the house greets *Shabbat* first by lighting candles in silver candelabra that adorn the dinner table. The father recites the *Kiddush* (wine benediction) and bread benediction (*Hamotzi*), then cuts the *Shabbat Challah,* and a full dinner is served. Following dinner, everyone joins in singing special songs that express the desire for peace that *Shabbat,* the Queen, inspires.

Traditional *Shabbat* foods have a very distinct personality: meals differ from those on week days in their lavishness and by the leisurely manner in which they are enjoyed. The dishes are prepared with special care and no expense or effort seems too big, as befits a very important occasion.

A Lavish Leisurely Dinner

Dinner on *Erev Shabbat* (Sabbath Eve) is composed of more courses than are usual during the rest of the week. It includes fish, soup, a main course with side dishes, dessert and occasionally tea with a piece of cake. It is not a hurried meal. The participants converse, sharing their experiences of the past week, with particular attention given to the children and their progress in school. Between courses and after the meal *Shabbat* songs are sung to enhance the relaxed, informal atmosphere.

Our menu for *Shabbat* is composed in the traditional spirit: *Gefilte Fish,* Beet Soup, Roast Chicken with Peas, Barley, Glazed Carrots and dessert. You can make it easy on yourself by spacing the cooking over two days and using some convenience foods.

Admittedly, the *Gefilte Fish* involves some extra work, but the effort is well worth it: the homemade product is far superior to anything you can buy. We suggest that you ask the man in the fish market to skin, filet and grind the fish for you, saving the skins and bones for your stock. Just be sure to have your fish on hand no later than Thursday if the *Gefilte Fish* is to be eaten on Friday. The second course, Beet Soup, can also be pre-

This table, set for a traditional Erev Shabbat (Sabbath Eve) dinner features, clockwise, from the top: BEET SOUP (recipe on page 118), GEFILTE FISH (recipe on page 117) and relishes. In front are a WHOLE ROAST CHICKEN (recipe on page 118), surrounded by green peas, and GLAZED CARROTS (recipe on page 119). On the left is the JIFFY FRUIT DESSERT (recipe on page 119) and just behind it a goblet and bottle of wine for the wine benediction.

pared a day in advance and will actually benefit therefrom: once chilled any extra fat in the soup will harden on the surface and can be lifted off easily.

On Friday all you have to do is put the chicken in the oven about two-and-one-half hours before dinner. While it roasts, you can do the Barley, fix the Glazed Carrots, assemble the Jiffy Fruit Dessert and set the table. About half-an-hour before dinner put the food on serving plates, heat the peas and put them around the chicken. Keep all the dishes in the turned-off oven that have to be served warm. They will keep well. Just before dinner arrange some relishes and pickles on a nice plate. Everything is now ready for greeting the *Shabbat*.

M E N U
(planned for 6 to 8)
Gefilte Fish*
Beet Soup*
Whole Roast Chicken*
Barley*
Glazed Carrots*
Green Peas
Relish Plate
Jiffy Fruit Dessert*
*Recipe given

GEFILTE FISH
(Photograph on page 116)

Literally *Gefilte Fish* means Stuffed Fish. Originally, fish were skinned, fileted, ground and mixed with other ingredients, then stuffed back in the skin of the hollow fish and cooked. The stuffing turned out to be so delicious without the skin that it is now served by itself, although the dish retains its traditional name. Horseradish-with-beets *(Chrain)* is usually also served to enhance the flavor of *gefilte fish*.

2 lb. carp
1 lb. whitefish
1 lb. buffalo fish
2 onions
3 tsp. salt
½ tsp. black pepper
2 tsp. sugar
2 slices white bread, toasted
3 tbls. bread crumbs
2 raw eggs
1 hard-boiled egg
2 drops almond extract

Fish stock:
6 cups water
3 carrots, sliced
2 onions, sliced
Parsley sprigs
Heads, skin and bones of the fish
2 tsp. salt
½ tsp. pepper
2 tsp. sugar

1. Buy 4 pounds of fish in the combination specified above. You may also buy other combinations of lake fish, but be sure to include carp. Ask the man in the fish market to filet the fish for you. Don't discard the heads and bones because you will use them for the stock. You may also ask him to grind the filets for you. Or, you can grind them at home, preferably with an electric grinder.

2. Prepare the stock: combine the water, sliced onions and carrots in a very large, shallow pot. Add parsley, seasoning, with the cleaned heads, skins and bones of the fish. Bring to a boil.

[117]

3. Soak the bread in a glass of water. Peel the onions and the hard-boiled eggs. Grind the fish. If they are already ground, put them in a large bowl. Grind onions and hard-boiled egg. Squeeze water out of the bread and grind it, too. Mix all of the ground ingredients together.

4. Add the salt, pepper, sugar, almond extract, raw eggs and bread crumbs. Mix well to combine all ingredients and flavors.

5. By now, the stock is boiling. Reduce the heat and shape fish in cakes: measure 1/4 cup of the fish mixture and form an elongated smooth cake with your hands. Put into the stock very gently. Repeat until you use all of the fish mixture. You will have about 12 large cakes.

6. Cover the pot and regulate the heat so there is a very slow simmer (medium-low or low). Simmer this way for 2 hours. Check occasionally. Taste, and correct seasoning, if needed.

7. Remove from heat. Lift the fish cakes and carrot slices from stock with a slotted spoon. Strain the stock through a fine sieve into a bowl. Pour some over the fish cakes and put the rest in a covered glass dish. Keep both in refrigerator. The stock will jell overnight.

8. To serve, place on a bed of lettuce leaves. Garnish with bits of beets and wedges of lemon dipped in snipped parsley. Have available the prepared horseradish with beets.

BEET SOUP
(Photograph on page 116)

A good, strong soup to prepare a day ahead and heat before serving.

    8 medium beets
    8 cups water
    2 carrots
    2 onions
    Small bunch of parsley
    2 celery stalks
    Back, wings and giblets of a chicken (1 lb.)
    1 tbls. salt
    1/8 tsp. pepper

1. Peel the beets, carrots and onions. Put them in a large pot with 8 cups of water. Add chicken pieces, except liver, salt and pepper.

2. Bring to a boil. After 10 minutes reduce the heat, cover and simmer for an hour. Add parsley and continue simmering for another hour. Taste and add salt, if needed.

3. Strain the soup into a large bowl. Cut 4 beets into strips and add to the clear soup. Serve hot. Use the remaining beets for Pickled Beets. (See index.)

WHOLE ROAST CHICKEN
(Photograph on page 116)

Our chicken is golden brown and crisp outside; juicy and delicious inside, and a most welcome main dish in a festive meal. Please read the entire recipe before you start, and plan to have the chicken done about half-an-hour before dinner so that you have time to prepare the wine sauce. Keep both warm.

    1 whole roasting chicken (5 to 6 lb.)
    3 tsp. salt
    1 tsp. sweet paprika
    1/2 tsp. pepper
    4 tbls. margarine

    Wine sauce:
    Pan juices
    1/2 cup white wine
    1 tbls. cornstarch
    1/2 cup water

1. Preheat the oven to 425°F.

2. Clean the bird thoroughly. Rub the skin and cavity with salt. Truss with strings to keep its shape during roasting. Sprinkle with pepper and paprika.

3. Put the bird on a rack in a shallow roasting pan. Roast for 30 minutes, breast up. Lower the heat to 375°F. and turn the bird to brown on the other side. Turn every 30 minutes until the bird is done.

4. Melt the margarine as soon as you put the bird in the oven. Baste the bird with the melted margarine and repeat several times during cooking to give the chicken a nice brown color. Use a brush or a basting bulb.

5. Roasting time is about 2 hours, and the bird is ready when the meaty portions are tender and the drumsticks feel soft when pressed between fingers, or when they move up and down easily at the joint.

6. Remove the bird from the oven. Cut and remove trussing strings. Put the chicken on a big serving platter and, if possible, keep warm in a turned off oven or food warmer.

7. To prepare the sauce, pour all the pan juices into a big measuring cup. Let stand several minutes so that all fat may rise to the top. Skim off the fat. Meanwhile pour the wine in the pan and stir all remaining brown bits to dissolve. Pour all the juice from the measuring cup and roasting pan into a saucepan and bring to a boil. Mix the water with the cornstarch and add to the boiling juices. Stirring continuously. Cook for 10 minutes on medium heat until the sauce is clear and thick.

BARLEY

A good starchy side dish that is a refreshing change from the more conventional potatoes and rice. It is also a well-liked traditional Jewish dish and most appropriate for the *Shabbat*.

    1½ cups barley
    3 cups hot water
    2 cubes chicken bouillon
    1 tsp. salt
    ⅛ tsp. pepper
    1 medium onion, chopped
    3 tbls. oil
    ¼ lb. mushrooms, chopped

1. Heat the oil in a large saucepan and lightly fry onion and mushrooms. Add the barley and fry together 5 minutes. Stir while frying.

2. Dissolve the bouillon cubes in the hot water and add to the barley with salt and pepper. Bring to a boil, then reduce the heat and cook slowly until all water is absorbed; about 45 minutes. Add a little water, if needed.

3. Before serving fluff up barley with a fork and bring piping hot to the table in a deep serving dish.

GLAZED CARROTS
(Photograph on page 116)

Carrots are very popular for festive meals because they add sweetness and color to the main dish. Our glazed carrots complement the Roast Chicken beautifully.

    2 lb. carrots
    3 tbls. margarine
    3 tbls. sugar
    1 tsp. cinnamon

1. Peel the carrots, clean them and cut crosswise, about ¼″ thick.

2. Boil in a large pot of salted water for 15 minutes, until they are tender.

3. Melt the margarine in a saucepan and add sugar and cinnamon. Drain carrots, add to saucepan and stir gently over medium heat until the carrots get a golden glaze, about 10 minutes.

JIFFY FRUIT DESSERT
(Photograph on page 116)

This is a real quick one. You use food from the pantry shelves and the only work left for you is assembling the ingredients and perking them up.

    1 1-lb. can pears
    1 1-lb. can sliced peaches
    1 4-oz. jar maraschino cherries
    2 tbls. fruit liqueur
    1 tbls. toasted coconut

1. Drain fruits, reserving syrup from peaches and pears. Arrange the peaches nicely in the center of a compote bowl. Place the pears, cut side up around them. Garnish with cherries, tucking one in each pear and piling the rest in center.

2. Mix the syrups. Add the liqueur and pour over the fruit. Sprinkle the center with toasted coconut.

A Make-Ahead Special Meal

The *Shabbat* day itself is one of rest for all the family, including mother. On this day no cooking is done, so mother is free of the kitchen. How can this be accomplished? Quite simply, as any experienced Jewish mother can tell you. The whole *Shabbat* midday meal is prepared in advance, ready to be served from oven or refrigerator. The cold dishes keep well without losing their flavor, while the hot ones invite the long, slow cooking that actually improves them tremendously. Together, they compose a delicious second feast, which is totally different in tastes and textures from the one eaten the night before.

Our menu for this make-ahead meal features an Egg-and-Onion Appetizer for openers. The second course, which is the hub of the *Shabbat* meal, is *Tcholent*, the Jewish Masterpiece. Meat, barley, potatoes and beans are the major ingredients of the *Tcholent*. This dish is rather easy to assemble and can be done well in advance. Traditionally, it is put in the oven on Friday afternoon and stays there until meal time. This long, slow baking blends flavors of all the ingredients which gives the *Tcholent* its wonderful aroma and deep, rich brown color. We serve Pickled Beets as a side dish and you may add other pickles and a salad. The only dessert that can be 'tolerated' after the *Tcholent* is a good, strong, hot glass of tea.

MENU
(planned for 6 to 8)

Egg-and-Onion Appetizer*
Pickled Beets
Tcholent,* The Jewish Masterpiece
Tea

*Recipe given

EGG AND ONION APPETIZER

A piquant and crunchy first course that really does its job as an appetizer and leaves everybody waiting for more food.

    6 hard-boiled eggs
    2 medium onions
    10 small radishes, grated
    ½ tsp. salt
    Dash of pepper
    3 tbls. chicken fat or salad oil
    Lettuce

1. Dice the onions in very small cubes and fry in chicken fat or salad oil until golden.

2. Chop the eggs and put into a bowl that can be tightly covered. Add the radishes to the fried onions and fat. Mix well, season with salt and pepper. Refrigerate covered until serving time.

3. Serve on a bed of lettuce or garnish with to-mato slices.

PICKLED BEETS

Pickled beets will add color to your table and zest to your dishes whether you serve them as a relish or as a salad. Plan on cooking them a day ahead because they should marinate overnight. For this dish you could use half of the beets from the Beet Soup (see index) Here, however, are complete instructions for preparing them from scratch.

    4 medium beets
    8 cups water
    2 tsp. salt

    Marinade:
    ½ cup oil
    4 tbls. vinegar
    2 tbls. lemon juice
    1 tsp. salt
    ½ tsp. sugar
    Dash pepper
    2 garlic cloves, mashed
    1 tbls. finely chopped onion

1. Clean and cook the beets, skins on, in a big pot with the water and salt, for about 40 min-utes, or until they are tender.

2. Remove skins under running water. They will come off very easily. Cut the beets in very thin slices or grate them on a coarse grater. Put into a dish that has a tight cover.

3. Make the marinade by mixing all the ingre-dients and stirring vigorously for 2 minutes. Pour marinade over beets and toss to cover everything. Cover dish and refrigerate overnight. Serve cold.

TCHOLENT, THE JEWISH MASTERPIECE

Tcholent is a classic Jewish dish, assembled the day before *Shabbat* so that it can be baked the whole night and still served hot, at the midday meal. *Tcholent* is eaten in a leisurely fashion to enjoy every bite—the best meal of the week.

    2 lb. pot roast meat, with some fat
    2 bones
    1½ cups beans, pre-soak them the night before using
    ½ cup barley
    2 onions
    3 lb. potatoes
    ½ cup oil
    2 tsp. salt
    ½ tsp. pepper
    1 tsp. paprika

1. Use a big, heavy pot with a tight-fitting lid. Brown the meat nicely in the pot with ¼ cup oil.

2. Chop the onions and brown them in a skil-let, using the remaining oil. Don't let them dark-en too much.

3. Use medium-sized potatoes. If you have big ones, cut them in half. See that the potatoes, or potato pieces, are of the same size.

4. Put the bones in with the meat into pot. Add the beans, barley and potatoes, arranging them nicely around the meat and bones. Sprinkle with seasoning and add the fried onions.

5. Cover with water. Bring to a boil on top of the stove, cover tightly and put into the oven. If you plan to bake the *Tcholent* overnight, which brings the best results, set thermostat at 250°F. Check occasionally and add water, if needed. The *Tcholent* is ready when it is brown, still moist and juicy, but not too watery.

6. Serve as a whole meal. Try it also as a main dish for a company hot buffet. For quicker cook-ing, bake at 350°F for 4 to 5 hours.

KASHRUT & KOSHER COOKING

THE JEWISH DIETARY LAWS

Kosher, or in its Hebrew form *Kasher,* literally means 'fit'. This word is used to describe the traditional ways of Jewish cooking. The Jewish dietary laws define very clearly what foods, ways of cooking, and serving are permitted. They are Biblical laws, interpreted by scholars, and observed for many centuries.

There are three classes of Kosher foods: Neutral *(Parve),* Dairy *(Milchik),* and Meat *(Flaishik).* Parve foods include all the vegetables, fruits and cereals. They also include kosher fish and other foods that are not dairy or meat. Shellfish and seafoods other than kosher fish are forbidden. Dairy foods are all those which originate from milk, or contain even a trace of a dairy product.

Meat foods come from specific animals. Prohibited are meats from mammals that the Bible considers 'unclean', such as pork. Even with the 'clean' animals (i.e. beef and sheep), only those are permitted that have been ritually slaughtered, then examined, and found perfect in their vital organs. The meat has to be further processed, with the blood and certain parts removed. Before cooking it has to be soaked in water and kept in salt, to extract the last traces of blood. For the same reason, liver has to be broiled.

Fowl belongs to the meat foods. The Bible lists a number of prohibited species (i.e. owls, ravens, etc.). Chicken, duck, turkey, and geese are kosher provided they are properly slaughtered, checked and prepared.

The Biblical law 'Thou shalt not cook the kid in its mother's milk' is the base for the separation of dairy and meat in the kosher kitchen. No meat or fowl are mixed, cooked, served or eaten with dairy foods, or vice versa. Observant Jews have two completely separate sets of dishes and utensils for cooking and serving meat or dairy foods. Neutral foods and fish can be served with either meat or dairy dishes.

There are additional dietary restrictions during the holiday of Passover. On this holiday no flour, bread or other leavened flour products are permitted. They should not even be in the house.

Using the Book for Kosher Cooking

MENUS AND RECIPES: This book complies with the Jewish dietary laws. It contains no forbidden ingredients or combinations in its recipes and menus. If you want to construct additional Kosher menus, use the Recipe Index, and pay attention to the designation given to each recipe. The recipes are marked either 'd' for Dairy, 'm' for Meat, 'p' for Parve. Dishes for Passover are marked with 'P.'

INGREDIENTS: To comply with the laws of *Kashrut* you have to start with kosher ingredients. Rabbinical supervision enables you to choose the right ones. Read labels carefully to determine if they contain meat or dairy products, and avoid mixing them. Please note that in this book all margarine called for is *Parve* margarine (contains no milk) and all gelatin is *Parve* too. During Passover all ingredients should be certified as *Kosher Le'Pessach.* All ingredients mentioned here are available in the United States.

GLOSSARY OF TERMS

AFIKOMAN: A piece of *Matzah* hidden as part of the *Seder* ceremony, 71.
ASHKENAZI: Jews whose origin is mainly Europe, 14.

————

BIKKURIM: 'The first fruit' in Hebrew. Referring to the ritual in ancient Israel of bringing the first fruit to the Temple, 105.
BLINTZE: (BLINTZES—pl.) A Jewish crêpe, 79, 106.
BUBALEH: 'Deary' in Yiddish. A sweet Passover pancake, 80.

————

CHALLAH: (CHALLOT—pl.) A braided or round egg-bread served on *Shabbat* and *Rosh Hashanah*, 9, 11.
CHRAIN: Ground horseradish with beets, 117.
CHREMSLACH: A traditional Passover soup dumpling, 73.

————

DEMI-TASSE: 'A half cup' in French. A small cup of black coffee served after a meaty meal.
DREIDEL: 'A top' in Yiddish. A toy played with during *Hanukkah*, 27.

————

EREV: 'Evening' in Hebrew. Jewish holidays start at the evening before, i.e. *Erev Shabbat* is on Friday night.
ETROG: A citrus fruit used during *Succot*, 22.

————

FALAFEL: Fried garbanzo beans shaped into balls, popular in Israel, 93, 96.

————

GEFILTE FISH: 'Stuffed Fish' in Yiddish. A Jewish classic dish, 117.

————

HAGGADAH: A special prayer book read on the *Seder* ceremony, 69.
HAG SAMEACH: 'Happy Holiday' in Hebrew. A common greeting during Jewish holidays, 88.
HAKAFOT: 'Going around' in Hebrew. The dancing and going around with the *Torah* scrolls in the synagogue on *Simhat Torah*, 23.
HAMANTASHEN: 'Pockets of Hamman' in Yiddish. A triangular, filled, small cake eaten on *Purim*, 48.
HAMISHAH ASAR: 'Fifteen' in Hebrew. Used in Yiddish as a term for dried fruits eaten on the 15th of *Shevat* (*Tu Bishevat*), 41.
HAMOTZI: 'who brings forth' in Hebrew. Blessing over bread, called after its first distinctive word, 10, 115.
HANUKKAH: 'Dedication' in Hebrew. Holiday celebrating the rededication of the Temple in ancient Jerusalem, 27-40.
HANUKKAH GELT: 'Money for *Hanukkah*' in Yiddish. Given as gifts to children on *Hanukkah*, 27.
HANUKKIAH: A special candelabra used during *Hanukkah*, 30.
HAROSET: A symbolic food set on the *Seder* table, 71, 73.
HUMMUS: A favorite Israeli dish, made of garbanzo beans, 93, 95.

————

IYAR: A Hebrew month in the beginning of summer, 91.

————

KABAB: Arabic name for elongated, ground meat patties, grilled on skewers, 102.

KASHER, KASHRUT: 'Fit' in Hebrew. Refers to the Jewish dietary laws, 122.
KIDDUSH: 'Sanctification' in Hebrew. Wine benediction, 10, 115.
KNEIDLACH: Passover soup dumplings, known also as *matzo balls*, 76
KOSHER: 'Kasher' in Yiddish. See above.
KOSHER LE'PESSACH: Foods fit for *Passover*, 69-90.
KREPLACH: Cooked soup dumplings, 20.
KUGEL: A slowly baked starchy dish, 74.
KUSHIOT: 'Questions' in Hebrew, asked by youngsters during the *Seder* ceremony, 71.

————

LAG BA'OMER: A one day holiday in early summer, 99-103.
LATKES: Traditional potato pancakes eaten during *Hanukkah*, 28, 31.

————

MAROR: Bitter herbs eaten in the *Seder* ceremony, 71.
MATZAH: (MATZOT—pl.) Special thin, crisp bread eaten on Passover, 69-90.
MATZO BALL: A Passover soup dumpling, 76.
MATZO MEAL: Ground *matzot*. A substitute for flour used during Passover, 73-90.
MEGILAH: 'A long narrow scroll' in Hebrew. Specifically referred to the Book of Esther which is read on *Purim*, 47.
MENORAH: 'A source of light' in Hebrew. Used as a term when referring to the sacred flame in the Temple in ancient Jerusalem, 27.
MISHLOACH MANOT: 'Sending of gifts' in Hebrew. A tradition of exchanging gifts of foods during *Purim*, 47.
MISHPOCHEH: 'Family and relatives' in Yiddish. Comes from the Hebrew word *Mishpachah*, meaning Family, 28.

————

NISAN: The Hebrew month of spring, when Passover takes place, 69.

————

PASSOVER: One of the major Jewish holidays, commemmorating the Exodus of the Jews from Egypt, 69-90.
PARVE: Food that is neutral, according to the laws of *kashrut*, 122.
PESSACH: The Hebrew name of Passover, 69-90.
PITAH: (PITOT—pl.) Flat round bread of the Middle East, 93, 96.
PONTCHEKES: Traditional fried cakes on *Hanukkah*, 31.
PURIM: A jolly holiday, occurring in early spring, 47-68.

————

RA'ASHAN: 'Noisemaker' in Hebrew. Used by children on *Purim*, 47.
ROSH HASHANAH: 'The head of the year' in Hebrew. The name of the New Year holiday, 9-16.

————

SEDER: 'Order' in Hebrew. Used as a term for the ceremony of welcoming Passover, 69-72.
SEPHARDIC: Jews whose origin was Spain, 14.
SHABBAT: The seventh day of the week, the day of rest, 115-121.
SHANAH TOVAH: 'A good year' in Hebrew. The traditional greeting on the Jewish New Year season, 9.
SHAVUOT: 'Weeks' in Hebrew, refers to a major holiday celebrated in summer, 105-114.

WEIGHTS AND MEASURES

This book is written according to the American system of weights and measures. In many cases, quantities are given both by weight and volume or package size.

In order to enable readers who live outside the U.S.A. to work with the book the following conversion factors are given. While they are not exact mathematical conversions, they are rounded in such a way as to make them easy to use.

OVEN TEMPERATURES

Description	°F	°C	Brit. Gas Mark	French Thermostat
Very slow	225	110	¼	2
	250	130	½	3
Slow	275	140	1	
	300	150	2	4
Moderate Low	325	170	3	
Moderate	350	180	4	
Moderate hot	375	190	5	5
	400	200	6	
Hot	425	220	7	6
	450	230	8	
Very Hot	475	240	9	7

EQUIVALENT MEASURES

American	Metric
1 oz.	25—28 gr.
1 lb.	450—500 gr.
1 tsp.	5 cc. = 5 ml.
1 tbls.	15 cc. = 15 ml.
1 cup	230—240 cc.
1 stick butter (4 oz)	100 gr.
1 inch	2.5 cm.

INDEX

[125]

RECIPE INDEX

Note: This index will help you in planning your own menus for many occasions. The recipes are coded to help in keeping the Jewish Dietary Laws. Dairy dishes are marked 'd'; meat dishes are marked 'm' and parve dishes are marked 'p.' To identify Passover dishes they have an additional 'P.'